A Healing Education

How Can Waldorf Education Meet the Needs of Children?

Five lectures given at the
West Coast Waldorf Teachers Conference
in Fair Oaks, California
February 15–19, 1998

Michaela Glöckler, M.D.

D1202627

RUDOLF STEINER COLLEGE PRESS

The publisher is grateful for the encouragement and support of Robert Dulaney in making publication of this book possible.

Cover art: Theodore Mahle
Cover design: Claude Julien, Hallie Bonde, and Theodore Mahle

ISBN 0-945803-48-6

Book orders may be made through Rudolf Steiner College Bookstore: Tel. 916-961-8729, FAX 916-961-3032.

Rudolf Steiner College Press
9200 Fair Oaks Boulevard
Fair Oaks, CA 95628

Editor's Foreword

These lectures are presented in the conversational style in which they were given. Dr. Glöckler regrets that she has not been able to give time to review and prepare these lectures for publication herself. However, she has urged that the content be made available as soon as possible. She has corrected a few items which were not clear in the tape recordings. Dr. Uwe Stave has reviewed the text and clarified the usage of medical terminology in English.

Many thanks to Astrid Schmitt-Stegmann, Jennifer Kleinbach, Felicitas Graf, Jürgen Flinspach, Ingun Schneider, and Hallie Bonde for their assistance in the preparation of the manuscript and the illustrations.

J.B.

Table of Contents

Preface

These lectures on health in education, given by Dr. Michaela Glöckler at the 1998 Waldorf Teachers Conference at Rudolf Steiner College, are a potent support for the work of the Waldorf teacher. As a physician, Dr. Glöckler can truly bring to the fore the physiological foundation of Waldorf Education, moving from clearly observable physical phenomena to the soul-spiritual forces working in them. This physiological approach supports the Waldorf teachers' striving for sensitive observation of each child and gives new perspectives for their grasp of the complicated nature of the human being. As these lectures were given to experienced teachers, an understanding of Rudolf Steiner's anthroposophical concepts is presumed.

Dr. Glöckler poses a question at the beginning of these lectures: Does this education still address the needs of our time and the children growing up in it? The topic of a healthy childhood for our children has been and is a burning question addressed by many writers such as Jerry Mander, Neil Postman, David Elkind, Joseph Chilton Pearce, Jane Healy, and many other prominent authors.

Doctors, educators, and therapists have a special need to meet the ever increasing illness manifesting on all levels in growing human individuals—be these attention deficit problems, behavior problems, sensory integration problems, psychosomatic disturbances, or genetic disturbances. Whatever the manifestations are, we must understand that underlying them are physiological problems. Dr. Glöckler points out that this understanding is fundamental to Waldorf Education. The key task for the educator, therefore, is to insure for the child a healthy physical development, for this is the basis for a healthy soul-spiritual development.

In the first lecture, Dr. Glöckler focuses on the "pedagogical law" given by Rudolf Steiner in *The Curative Education Course* (also published as *Education for Special Needs*). She illumines the comprehensiveness of this law, the insight it offers into the workings of the fourfold human nature, and the karmic effects of this fourfold working from one life to another. She then takes us on a path that starts with the physical body, pointing out some of the wonders of embryological development and then bringing to our consciousness further growth rhythms of the brain and other organs. She demonstrates the difference between human and animal and shows how, in the animal, wisdom and intelligence have formed the physical body and express themselves through instinct. She opens new doors of understanding for the teacher that can lead him or her to grasp more clearly the significance that the releasing of intelligence from the body plays in human development.

Dr. Glöckler points to an "instinct deficiency" in the human being that is necessary for human freedom. This deficiency has, however, to be compensated for by intelligence. In order not to lose our humanity, education must replace the lack of instinct. In the third lecture the theme of the freeing of the etheric forces is led further so that we can see the various subtle gestures and qualitative differences in the thought formation and thinking activity, and how these show the characteristic of the specific organs from which they were released.

In the course of these lectures we receive extraordinary help and support to recognize not only the working of the etheric in its transformation into the formative, creative activity of thinking, but we also learn to feel our way into the many wonderful rhythms that the astral forces, the musical forces, use to penetrate the human body. The ego organization then stands before us as the great integrator.

To nurture this development from physical to soul-spiritual, there is no Waldorf Education without the arts. Why? There are, of course, many reasons. We can learn to see the human being as a revelation of all the arts, actually constructed out of their different laws. In the fourth lecture we are guided to deeper insights and understandings of the mission of the arts in their connection with the sevenfold human being. It becomes ever clearer to us that it is a travesty to deprive the growing human being of a living involvement with the different arts. The healing and harmonizing effect of the arts is a bulwark against violence and aggression; in addition the arts bring health into the whole constitution of the growing child, right down into the formation of the physical body.

We thank Dr. Glöckler for the wealth of insight that she has given us in these lectures. Educators, artists, and therapists connected to Waldorf Education will treasure the many indications that can stimulate them to further discoveries.

—Astrid Schmitt-Stegmann

Lecture 1: The Pedagogical Law and its Expression in Karma and Reincarnation

Sunday, February 15, 1998

Good evening, dear friends of Waldorf Education, an education which loves the human being. I was first here in Sacramento thirty-seven years ago. It was 1961 and I remember how impressed I was. I was a high school student and I had the chance to visit the Sacramento Waldorf School for about a week in the ninth grade. My experience at the time was that the students were so *nice* compared to what I knew from Europe. I came away with a picture of American students and especially Waldorf school students as having an endless respect for their teachers. When the teacher came in, the students would be sitting there as if expecting something important, and then the lesson would begin. People called each other by their first names, and this was also astonishing for a European. Now when I remember back to this situation and then look at how time has changed and how we read in the newspapers all the statistics about learning disabilities, learning difficulties, and behavior disturbances on this continent as well as in Europe, one really must say that this time-space of a full generation, not only thirty years but thirty-seven, is really a time-space which has changed the world completely. We have totally different adults, totally different children. But Waldorf Education is still here, and the question which arises—must arise—is: Are the principles of this education still as modern as they were thirty-seven years ago, and seventy-eight years ago, at the founding of the first Waldorf School? This is the first question: *Does the essence of this education really address modern times?*

A second basic topic I would like to look at right in the beginning concerns the fact that *the great change in behavior reflects a change in health.* The children I remember here in the sixties were more or less healthy children from a doctor's point of view. And in our times we must say that healthy children are becoming ever more rare, something special. We have many physical problems connected with the skeletal system. We also have many problems in the realm of cognition: attention deficit problems, problems of ability, behavioral problems. Increasingly doctors are discovering physiological disturbances as the basis for all these problems: brain disturbances, genetic disturbances, and disturbances of the physical body. However, once one has found a physical problem to be the so-called origin or reason for an illness or disturbance, this does not mean that one can't do anything about it. Treatment is still a big question, but it is very important to understand that behind every behavior and disturbance problem there must be a physiological problem. And this is, interestingly, the basic idea of Waldorf Education.

Study of Man laid the basis for Waldorf Education in 1919 [lecture series also published as *The Foundations of Human Experience,* Hudson, New York: Anthroposophic Press, 1996]. This first big lecture cycle Rudolf Steiner gave on Waldorf Education deals with the development of soul forces and the physiological precondition for this development. For Rudolf Steiner it was completely clear that one cannot have healthy behavior, nor a healthy development of thinking, feeling, and willing capacities of soul, nor healthy spiritual forces, if one cannot create the physical conditions needed for such development. We have from the very beginning an education which focuses first on the body and secondarily on soul and spirit. That's interesting. So from the point of view of health, Waldorf Education is still the most modern education in existence because it educates the body first as the basis for soul and spiritual development. It is a health-oriented education. This is tremendously important especially in modern times. So the second question is: *What sort of health-oriented education do we*

*need, and how can we discover this health-orientation in Waldorf
education so that we can help the children of today?*

There is yet a third aspect I would like to focus on, and that
is the signature of our time. We are at the end of the twentieth
century preparing for the twenty-first. I would like to intro-
duce this signature of our time with a question from a German
ethical philosopher, a Jewish philosopher by the name of Hans
Jonas. He lived with this question as he was going through the
horrible experience of his mother's dying in Auschwitz. Jonas
asked himself: *Where was God when the atrocity at Auschwitz
hapened?* It was for him an existential question. And I'm sure
that in speaking about this question he spoke out of the hearts
of many people who share it. In the twentieth century there has
been a steady process of people leaving the churches in a way
no century before has seen. It is interesting that in Europe last
year was the first year in the twentieth century in which this
exponentially growing process of leaving the church stopped.
For the first time the number of people leaving started to dip
rather than to increase. There seems to be the beginning of a
change in the relationship to the spiritual world, and we can
only hope that what we call religious life will change so that
we can move to a new kind of spiritual life that we don't yet
have. A change is happening, but it is not yet clear which way
it will go.

But back to Hans Jonas. He lived with this question and
many, many people live with it. It has come in this century
whenever there have been wars, cruelty, and overwhelming
problems of a dimension that mankind did not experience in
earlier centuries. This question—What about God?—has gone
deeper and deeper. Hans Jonas found an answer for himself.
He realized that if there is a God he cannot be all-wise, he cannot be the one who knows everything and who has this knowing in conjunction with an almighty power over everything.
He realized that Auschwitz could not have happened if God
were all-wise, for then he would have seen it coming and
would have stopped it. And also, God cannot be almighty,
because if he were almighty Auschwitz would likewise not

have happened. *So what is God without omniscience and almighty power?* And then Jonas saw that there is one sublime power which does not focus on wisdom or power but which is something different, and that is love. He realized that between the realm of wisdom and the realm of will with its power there is a middle sphere, the sphere of love. It is this force that unites God and human beings totally, not wisdom, not power. The human being must be able to step out of God's wisdom and must be able to step out of God's power. Therefore God is no longer almighty in wisdom and power because the human being can step out of this and create something like Auschwitz. But the sphere of love still unites the human being and God completely, and therefore the answer Hans Jonas found to his own question was: God was present in Auschwitz. Love is able to develop a tremendous compassion which overcomes suffering.

It is very interesting that Hans Jonas came to this answer, because I know many people, and I'm sure you do too, who doubt God's existence as they face the problems of our time and look back at our horrible wars. But the people who lose their relationship to God can realize that there is only one possibility of finding him again, and that is to develop love. Without love we cannot understand the phenomenon *God.* If we have only wisdom and power, we cannot understand God. We can only find doubts and questions. We can even come to say, like the king of Spain: If I were the creator of the world, the world would be simpler. We cannot understand why everything is so complicated.

This is the third question that I would like to bring into our conference on the theme of how to educate the children of our time so that they can create the world of tomorrow: *Can we come to a deeper understanding of this time?* —especially when we look at such a magic number as 1998, if we see it together with the story in the Apocalypse and bring it together with the number of the beast, 666—which, as described in the Apocalypse of Saint John, is the expression, the imagination of evil, of the power of evil. How can we come to an understanding of the evil soul, as Hans Jonas did? How can we discover that evil has something to do with mankind's development in the very central point of decision? The human being definitely has the disposition to develop the faculty of freedom, and this is the crucial point of everyone's development. How do we deal with our own freedom and with the freedom of the other? And how is freedom thinkable without the existence of error—without the existence of evil? This is a most painful thought, that evil has to be in the world as a condition of human development. If this human development is to include freedom, then as more and more people develop this faculty of freedom, we must find a way to deal with the power of evil in our education system and not to wonder or be surprised if children—and also we teachers, we adults—start to become more and more difficult. We must realize that this is the signature of modern times, of emancipation, of times in which humankind first realizes that freedom is really the condition—even the freedom to leave God, to leave the churches, why not? This is a real expression of humanity's development, that freedom is becoming a reality, an individual reality. This is new.

In ancient Greek times, freedom had only a political dimension, it was not yet an individual faculty. This individual freedom is developing now, which means that every human being—and it starts already in childhood in our times—has to face the problem of evil. So we need an education in which evil can be faced and integrated, can be found as something we need, as a resistance, something to help us to wake up to how serious every human being's development really is.

Rudolf Steiner was often asked by members of the Anthroposophical movement what his life's task was, and he gave two answers. One of his tasks, he said, was to bring the knowledge of reincarnation and karma, to develop this knowledge, and to do research on this matter. His second task was to show individuals the path of initiation so that they could discover that the mission of evil in the world is to awaken human beings to their path of initiation. The mission of evil in the world is not to bring human beings under its power, but rather to awaken human beings to what is human so that they might overcome evil.

And this was the task Rudolf Steiner saw for himself, to go through this initiation, and so he did. And from a pedagogical point of view that is most wonderful. He lived in such a way that wherever he met a problem, he answered this problem with a positive initiative. When we meet problems, we usually start to criticize, or we just ignore them, or we question a lot, but it is not very common to answer something problematic with a fresh, positive initiative. Yet this is exactly what is most helpful for a teacher's development and biography, to face every provocation of a pupil with an attitude of positive initiative.

We have three themes before us. There is a major shift in the behavior of children and a growing tendency in our time to struggle with the power of evil. We who are educators and helpers of children must find a way to see this delicate process of a young person's physical and spiritual development as the field of our daily work. We must work to help physical development occur in such a way that a healthy soul and spiritual development can result. And that's the theme of this conference, this middle theme of the three I mentioned. I hope that we can discover how to create such an educational process. I hope also that we can bring this path of education in such a way that we adults and educators can experience it as a stimulus for us as well, which gives us the possibility to develop ourselves further.

I mentioned the question of the life task with which Rudolf Steiner lived. Of course, we can all live with the question: What is my task? The further question of every good teacher is: What is the task of the human beings who are sitting in my class, and what can I bring that will help them to develop, to meet their destiny, to meet their task? So when Rudolf Steiner said, answering this question, that his most important task was to bring a new insight into reincarnation and karma, then we might say that in our time we all need to work on this task. We teachers have begun to work with it. We all need to become something of a researcher in the field of reincarnation and karma. For Rudolf Steiner it was his life's task, and for most of us I think it may not be our whole life task, but for all of us it is part of our life task to understand how the developmental process of the human being unfolds if we realize that these human beings, the students who are sitting in front of us, are not living on the earth for the first time. And therefore we are giving these lectures for this conference dealing with reincarnation and karma in a special way, in the way that Rudolf Steiner calls the *pedagogical law*.

The pedagogical law is a way to look at reincarnation and karma from a pedagogical point of view, a way which I would like to characterize as the path of experience. We have in our time quite a lot of experimental reincarnation research, even a lot of forms of diagnosis and treatment in that field. But the way Rudolf Steiner did karmic research was very different. He entered into reincarnation and karma research by observation and thinking and not at all by suggestion and hypnosis, in which people become loose and lax. There are many different pathways for entering into the realm of the unconscious, the realm in which the knowledge and wisdom of previous lives can be discovered. But if we enter directly into this realm of the unconscious by methods of relaxation and hypnosis, methods of being guided by the voice of a therapist—just close your eyes, and then you have certain music, and then you let go, what do you see? what do you feel? . . . If we just follow and give ourselves in a certain sense into the hands of the guide, then we come into relationship with a guru who guides our inner life in a certain direction, but we are not sure if this is really the way to come to our proper being.

There are so many things living in the unconscious that it is very difficult to discriminate between my own previous destiny and that of my friends. It is difficult to discriminate between things that I have heard about or read and things I have experienced myself. The whole network of human relationships lies in my unconscious and comes out, creating pictures. So there is a high probability of coming into illusion, into pictures which don't really meet my own reality. This is not at all the way Rudolf Steiner entered into this field of research. His method was rather to observe and to think. In this way we use the faculty in which we as human beings are most awake, most aware, most clear. The pedagogical law describes it as a way into self-experience starting with observation and thinking. This pathway is most helpful for teachers.

I would like to give an introduction to this pedagogical law so that this evening before going to sleep you can do a little self-observation and self-research, which we can build on tomorrow. How can we come to a certain realization of our earlier lives? What sort of self-observation can we start with if we want to have an insight that is not at all suggestive, but that leaves us free? What gives me some certainty that I am on solid ground? Here it is helpful to realize that we have a sphere of *I* experience. When you listen to me, you are living in the present. You are listening, you are following these introductory remarks and thoughts not yet knowing quite where they will lead, and you may be thinking something or other at the same time or taking notes. You are living in the present. This is the sphere of our ego in which our *I* is always active. It is the power with which we are fresh and open, not bothered by the past. We are simply awake, living in thoughts. It is awareness, it is attention. Ego experience is attention experience. Attention deficit disorder, ADD, is a problem in which we strive to regain our full ego capacity. People who struggle with this syndrome struggle to regain their ego presence, and they suffer from a partial lack of this presence. When the ego is present, we can concentrate, we can look at something with the warmth of attention in the present.

Then we come to a lower sphere of self-experience, to our astrality, our soul with its life of thinking, feeling, and willing, our emotional life, our life of drive, and our memories in which certain ideas are fixed. This is the sphere of self-experience in which we meet the past and ideas of the future. Here we meet our fear, our hope, our hate, and we feel an already created world-reality. This world is not fresh and open. It is astonishingly fixed with prejudice, with experience from the past—it was so-and-so, so now I hesitate to trust him. This is a very interesting world in which we also find a certain basic need in our soul. Some people express it in terms of music, saying: There is a basic melody of my life, there is a certain mood in my soul life which is rather more melancholic, or rather more light-filled, which is more heavy or dissonant or consonant. This life melody is created out of these qualities of thinking, feeling, and willing that we carry in our soul.

There is a huge difference between the sphere of attention and this sphere of formed and, in a certain sense, fixed modalities. We can also experience a certain struggle when the ego, the *I* capacity of our actual will and attention, starts to question fixed thoughts and starts to work on the emotions. Sometimes we experience the battle of fighting against certain emotions that we have but don't want. Or we wish to have feelings that we don't have. Where does this come from? On the one hand there is an intensive interaction, and on the other hand, a remarkable resistance. We try to change something, but we feel there is a great resistance and that change is very hard work.

And then below that, we experience a third level, the level of our life habits or customs. What in our life is produced or stimulated by our habit life? How many people feel they would like to do something or have excellent ideas but then don't act on them because the life of their habits is so strong that they hesitate or they are afraid even to step forward. How big is the role habit plays in when we get up in the morning, how we have our room at home, what we like to do every day? Many people hesitate to change something in their lives because they feel as if they would lose part of their identity if they had to move to another country or another profession, for example. Others feel this less strongly. Some are bound by their customs more than others. It is a sphere which has a huge influence on life decisions, and it is very important to ask myself what role my life of customs and habits plays in my basic behaviors. The fact that my habitual behavior is this way and not that way can create turning points in destiny. It is more difficult to change something in this sphere because the resistance coming from habit life is still stronger than the resistance coming from the soul sphere.

Finally, we have a fourth level, the physical. At the physical level we feel we are constructed in a particular way, that we are limited. The sphere of the physical forces is the sphere of our limits. Even if we have the best habits, the most flexible soul, and a huge amount of attention, if there is a lack of physical ability we will not be able to do what we want. When you walk, the length of your steps is a certain distance which depends on the length of your legs. And if you look from this point of view at your karma, can you remember meetings or experiences which depended on the length of your legs? Perhaps you came to a certain place at just the moment to meet another person whom you would have missed seconds or minutes later. And you could only meet him because you were walking at a certain speed in your size of physical body.

The physical condition of our body creates karmic situations. And of course how we meet the physical body plays quite a role in this drama: who likes whom, old, young, the sexes, the whole appearance, the impression—and there we are mostly fixed. When we try to change something on the physical level, we experience the biggest resistance. But of course, we change. If we work for years, for example in the field of eurythmy, we can change the way we move, the way we walk. We can bring our physical body into a different form. We can handle it much better than without that training, but it needs years of study. And what does all this have to do with karma?

If we analyze ourselves in the sphere of attention and ego-presence and ask ourselves: What are the moments in which I am really present? What is my ego interested in? Where do I live when I am fully attentive? Then we realize that we come from a certain standpoint, perhaps with limited interests. But we realize, too, that all of our personal motivation depends on this ego sphere, that we have the possibility, if we wish, to be interested in everything. We can experience that this ego sphere of awareness and possible attention is the most open and flexible sphere. It is the sphere of unlimited possibility. In the other spheres we experience more and more limits. Where do these limits come from? The archetype of the soul—thinking, feeling, and willing—is an unlimited thing. In our thought life we have the possibility to understand all. In the life of our feeling we have the possibility to feel compassion for everything. And with our will we have the possibility to learn and to develop any faculty. But in our self-exploration we experience that we are limited on the soul level, and it is there that we meet our own personal karma from the previous life. What we meet as limits on the soul level in this life are the results of our ego-awareness in the last incarnation, our attention, our interest. The limitation we experience in this life in the sphere of the astral body is the concrete, realistic memory—or we can also say an imprint—of the presence of our ego activity throughout the previous life. In this life we are open, free, and unlimited in the ego-sphere because the imprint of all the bad and good experiences in the last life has passed into the current astral body. So when we don't like something in the sphere of the astral, we are meeting the signature of our ego activity in our last life.

Take these as questions for this evening as you look at your soul's melody: Is there not something like a refrain, like a memory of the configuration of my destiny, of the biography of my last life? And do I meet it now in the way my life's melody, my soul limitations, show me a certain signature of my own?

Then study your habits and explore them, and ask yourself what the imprint in this sphere is. Live with the question: Might it be that the specific limits I meet in this life in the sphere of my life forces and habits are the imprint of my astral (soul) activity in the last life?

And could the way I meet my physical body with its limits and its form be the imprint of the way my behavior and customs were established and carried me through my previous life?

This exercise begins merely as a question, as a kind of hypothesis even. But it can turn to a reality when we realize how self-education works, for any sort of self-education works this way. You start out of the flexibility and the freedom of your ego awareness, and you pay attention to and work on a certain task or a certain faculty you would like to develop. To do this you need your will, your feeling, your motivation, and your thoughts to understand it in working it through. So if you do any sort of self-education, you need first to educate your soul because you need your soul forces to make any progress. But if you work on your soul and develop a certain faculty, this will sooner or later change your habits, change your life's behavior. And if your life's customs and habits change, the conditions of your physical life and body will also change, although this takes the longest. By working on self-education in this way that Rudolf Steiner suggests we can have a remarkable experience of the pedagogical law at work, going through the astral and the etheric spheres and ending up in a physical reality, in a physical change.

And one life is the educator of the next. The same sequence applies. My engagement in the ego sphere, in the sphere of my *I* forces, determines the destiny of how my astral body will develop and be penetrated by the ego forces. My humanity is revealed through my thinking, feeling, and willing; the signature of my ego activity penetrates the astral so that the astral becomes more and more human. And the more humanly my soul activity is developed, the more this will appear in the realm of my behavior and customs. My whole life's struggle with my soul gives the condition of my etheric constitution in my next life. How I deal with my astral body today not only transforms my current life of customs and habits but also prepares the way it will be formed in the next life.

Human development moves from inside out. It starts in the inner warmth and intensity of the *I*, penetrates the sphere of the astral, transforms the sphere of the etheric with all its resistance of habit, and finally ends up in the physical. So we are active in the present life, in a second life in which the memory of ego-activity is in the astral, and in a third life in which I carry this memory in my etheric. And in the physical body of the present I carry the results of three earlier lives. So in every moment if we do a little self-exploration and self-experience, we can discover qualities, signatures, fashions in the spheres of our self-experience which come from our previous lives and become opened to our observation and self-knowledge. And we can experience a fifth life in everything we meet as our destiny. Today the fact that we meet here in this wonderful hall is part of all of our destinies. We are lucky to have the possibility in this special year, to meet in this hall, and this will change something in all of our lives—depending on how we meet, how we sleep, which ideas really become important for us, which do not, and so on. And what we meet and how we meet attracts our attention and involves our ego activity, and so this circle closes. How I behave with my physical deeds comes back to me in my next life as destiny. That we meet here is the result of the destiny that we prepared physically in our last life. The way we meet conditions now can carry the whole destiny process a positive step forward.

So every teacher carries in his or her constitution five lives with their destinies. Every pupil has the same—and now two destinies, with all these qualities and memories of previous lives, meet. And for the student, the teacher is a tremendous factor of destiny on whom he depends greatly. This is why Rudolf Steiner calls it the pedagogical law in the Curative Course. For self-education and for karmic law, we described how what lives in one sphere goes one step lower in the next incarnation. This law also works between a teacher and his students. How the teacher meets the student in the present with his attention and with his warmth creates and forms the student's astral body. The child is not yet able to educate himself because the full ego capacity is not there. The teacher replaces the ego in a certain sense, and his ego has a direct influence on the student's astral body.

Similarly, the way the teacher's astral body is formed with its resistance, with its lacks, in the sphere of thinking, feeling, and willing, educates enormously the life sphere of the pupil. The way the teacher brings out his soul activities is received by the student's etheric body, in the good and in the bad sense. If a child is a bit anxious and hesitant, day after day, week after week, month after month, year after year, this creates habits of behavior in his life. The way you work with your soul has a strong influence on the student's etheric body. And the way you behave, the way your habits work, starting and ending the lesson in a certain fashion, or taking a break in the middle of the lesson when it seems necessary, has a great influence on the student's physical constitution.

So this very briefly introduces the essence of the pedagogical law. The human being is very flexible but differentiated, and just through the way we are, we have a tremendous educating influence on our students, on the children we work with. I beg you to reflect on this a little, and then we will work concretely with it tomorrow. Thank you for listening so well this evening. I know many of you have also come from far away. I hope you will sleep well, and I'll see you tomorrow.

Lecture 2: The Image Character and Language of the Physical Body

Monday, February 16, 1998

Today I would like to address the theme of education and health more from a physical point of view. I mentioned yesterday that the basis of Waldorf education is that throughout kindergarten, the grades, and high school, students are always engaged in one activity in addition to whatever else they are busy with, and that is their physical growth. For Rudolf Steiner this principle was the most important thing to teach the teachers.

It has become increasingly clear over the course of this century just what this means, namely that absolutely everything which comes to the child's senses—even when it is still in its mother's body—has a stimulating effect on his physical constitution. Even now when I am speaking to you, you are in a different physical state from the one you would be in if I spoke very fast. The speed of my speech has a different effect on your breathing, even on your heartbeat. This is not a big problem for you as adults, because your body is full-grown and fully formed. It has more of a functional effect on you than a constitutional one because your constitution has acquired a certain solidity. But everything—how we treat the child and the way in which we bring certain effects to the child—affects and influences its growing process as such.

To begin with I would like to give an overview of physical development. This is the basis for everything we do as teachers to stimulate the physical constitution so that later the soul and spiritual activity and the human being's inner life can develop. How we stimulate the body and how the body is then the carrier of the revelations of soul and spiritual activity is the secret of education.

Head

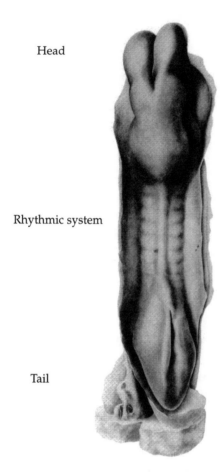

Rhythmic system

Tail

Human embryo
3 ½ weeks

First I would like to show some slides to illustrate how the growing process during pregnancy takes place. This human embryo is three millimeters long and three-and-a-half weeks old. Even at three weeks we can see that the threefold order of the body is already clearly developed. We have here the rhythmical constitution of the vertebrae which reaches into the tail section. It is an amazing phenomenon that the threefold order is really *the* basic order of human existence.

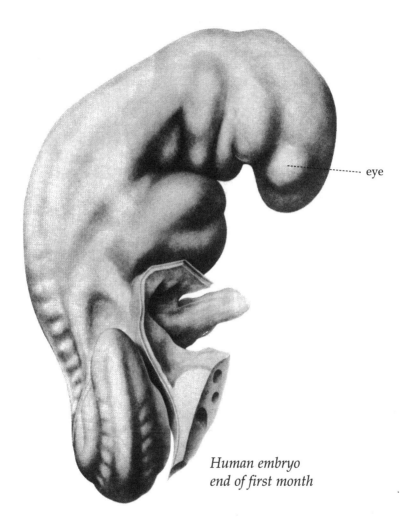

eye

Human embryo
end of first month

One week later in the fourth week of development the embryo is three-and-a-half millimeters long, and we see how fast the head constitution is growing. We can even see the beginning of the eye formation, and the wonderful rhythmic forms now manifesting in the caudal region. One also gets an impression of what Rudolf Steiner means when he speaks about the etheric forces as modeling, plastic forces.

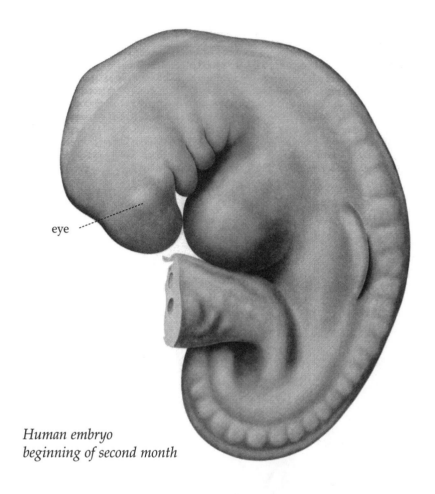

eye

Human embryo
beginning of second month

Now we have the fifth week of development, the beginning
of the second month. Week by week there is an enormous
change, and now we have clearly the head and the lower part
and the middle part. We see too that the head and tail are
approaching one another. This is another mystery we must
touch on this week: why is there first the wonderful straight
position starting at three weeks, and then why do we have the
gesture of the head and tail almost forming a circle? There is
room enough to be in a swimming position, so from that point

of view there is no reason for this rounding to exist at all. Taking this circle position is something which lies in the growing activity itself. In the delicate first two months of development all the organ functions begin to be established. We call this the embryonic period. Later, the time from the third month to the end of pregnancy, when the organs are only growing, is called the fetal period.

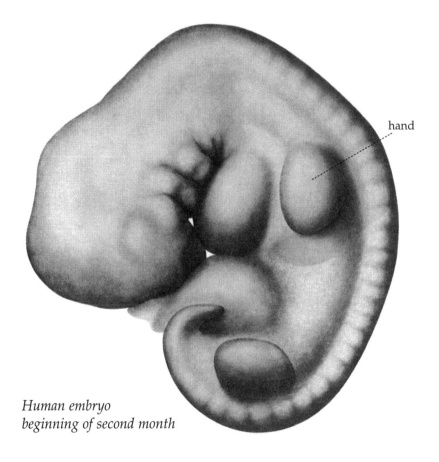

hand

Human embryo
beginning of second month

Here again we have the fifth week. From this vantage point we can see how the hands and arms are starting to form very delicately.

20

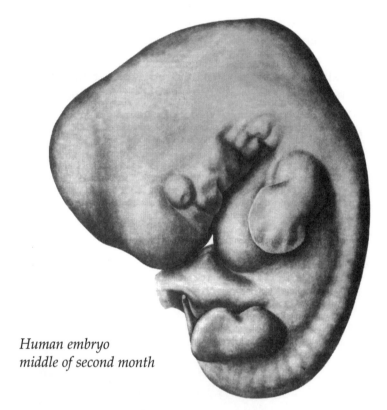

Human embryo
middle of second month

And here we have the sixth week, and you see how quickly the embryo is developing. Week by week there is enormous progress. You can see now not only how the hand is growing out as the first aspect of the limbs, but also how the feet are coming out. We see this archetypal picture that Rudolf Steiner speaks of in *Study of Man*. He says there that our limb system is created from the periphery, and we can see from the embryology that this is true. Limb development starts with the most peripheral structures, with fingers and toes. Later on, the lower part of the arm develops, and the last is the upper part. Therefore, years ago when the thalidomide catastrophe was happening all over the world, we saw three or four fingers attached to the shoulder because in this delicate period at the beginning of pregnancy, if there is a halt to development, then the growing process has to stop at the stage where it was. At the fifth or sixth week only the fingers are developed or a bit of the lower arm, and we saw this in those cases of malformation arising out of this inhibition during early pregnancy.

And we see here how close the head and tail are now, that the circle is almost closed. These pictures are extremely exact, taken from real embryos and enlarged by a professor of anatomy and embryology named Blechschmidt. His pictures and models are quite famous; he mounted a huge exhibit of every organ growing as it does in nature.

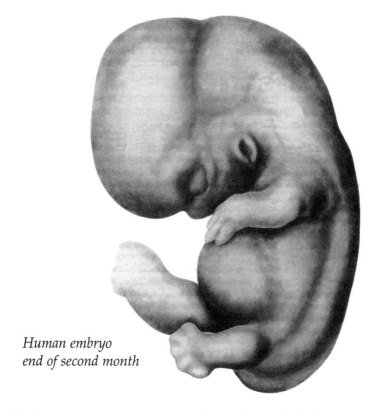

Human embryo
end of second month

And now we have a picture from the end of the second month, the seventh or eighth week of development. The embryo's length is about one-and-a-half centimeters. At this stage you see the fingers and the feet and the beginning of the lower legs. You can see here the already extremely well developed head, the ear and eye, the liver, and the heart under the hand. The baby has its hand on its heart. If you model this afternoon in the clay modeling course, you will see that this is a wonderful modeling process. The etheric body is the archetypal modeler of physical substance. At this time everything is a gel, transparent, not yet mineralized. All these forms first work in the liquid state, and only later, in the fifth or sixth month, does mineralization rapidly take place.

When the child is born we have the extremely delicate first three months in which Sudden Infant Death Syndrome can occur. During this delicate period the child again has to make a certain decision: Do I really want to live? It is similar to the first three months of development *in utero* during which miscarriages often happen. So, interestingly, the first three months of pregnancy are very delicate and then also the first three months of postnatal life are tenuous. We call this time the two delicate first trimesters.

During these first three months the nervous system in the brain also develops very quickly. Right after birth there is very little differentiation in our brain's cortical structures, but all those nerve cells grow very rapidly, making contact with one another through their dendrites. In the initial three months of life there is a marvelous plasticity in growing and finding and networking. Three months! That is extremely rapid.

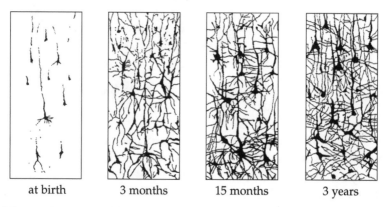

| at birth | 3 months | 15 months | 3 years |

Microscopic sections of the human cerebrum showing synapses between brain cells

The first three months in which this networking imprint begins is the period most vulnerable to outside influences. Through the rest of the first year the changes are still very great, and then in the second, third, and fourth years, they gradually decrease. A little of the plasticity of the brain system remains with us through all of life because the human being is a learner. We never become adult as animals do. When an animal becomes mature, it knows everything that it must know for its life, whereas when we pass puberty, none of us knows. That is the great difference between the human being and the animal. To make clear how delicate and vulnerable this growing process is as we will compare the human being and the animal, I would like to show you some more pictures.

This is the skeleton of the jumping mouse. This mouse is able to jump very far, and you see how small the arms are while its hind legs and tail are quite large. You can really see from the skeleton how fixed and specialized the form of the mouse's body is. This is typical of every kind of animal. The animal's physical body is well-formed and well-prepared for all the activities and functions of its life. It therefore reveals its behavior with great perfection through its body. Throughout his life the human being, by contrast, remains childlike and unspecialized in form.

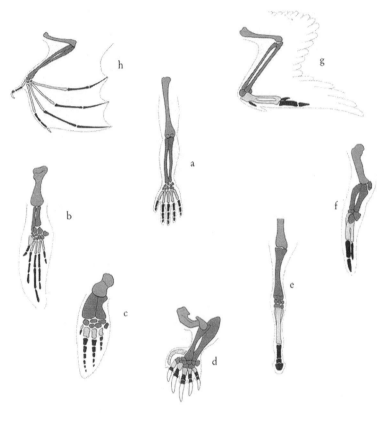

a. human   b. sea turtle   c. dolphin   d. mole   e. horse
f. penguin   g. bird   h. bat

You can see here how differentiated the limb formations are in these different animals. Feel your human arm and hand, and now compare it with the bird and the cow and all these animals with their greatly specialized limb formations.

The human being remains unspecialized. We can see this archetypally if we look at the development of the animal at the embryological and young stages. This picture of chimpanzees is very famous. We see on the right the wonderful adult form in which the skull is very flat and the muzzle is very prominent. In the middle, at a younger stage, it looks somewhat more like a human being. In the newborn on the left, the chimpanzee has the form of a human baby—the high forehead and the wonderfully formed back of the head and the verticalization of the face. The human face is vertical. In an animal, to smell and to sense and to make sounds and to eat and to act with the lower, mobile parts of the face—this all protrudes forward, in front of the thinking part of the head. We human beings have the same verticality and threefoldness in our face that we have in all our uprightness: all the organs are oriented below the head. So we see that the human being is constituted so that the head is on top and has to say where to go, and everything else is subordinated. In the animal it is different. There we see the strong guiding power of the will, of the activity. The head and the brain function follow the will.

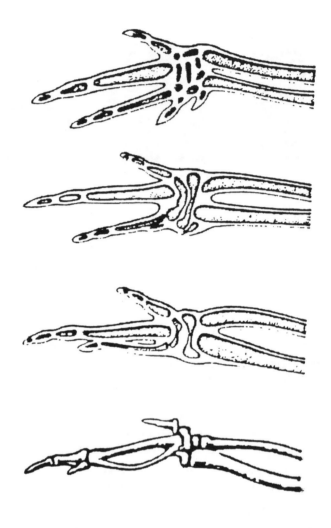

We can watch a similar miracle of the growing process in, for instance, the arm of any vertebrate. Here I'll show you the development of the arm of a bird. In the beginning of the embryological development of the bird (at the top), we can still see the five fingers of the hand. By the next stage, two of the fingers have been obliterated and only three fingers are left. Then in the third stage, we see that the remaining fingers are becoming immobile and two of them come nearer and nearer to one another. And finally these two fingers have come together. The middle finger grows the longest until you have a wonderful flying skeleton in which the wings are well prepared and the fingers serve the flying process. There is no need for a bird to have an opposable thumb because it doesn't need to do all the activities that we can do with our hands; in the bird there is a sacrifice of great range of activity in order to serve this one specialized function of flying.

When we compare the human being with the animal, it is important to see that in animals the whole skeleton during embryological development first produces a human-like form and then specializes into a particular animal form. From this one can understand the error in Darwinism of placing the human being at the end of the sequence of development. Rather, by looking at embryological development one sees that the human form comes first and that all animals are specialized human beings. There is of course a relationship between the human being and the animal, but it is the reverse of what is usually supposed. There are some class teachers here, so I would like to share a brief anecdote.

When I worked as a school doctor, I had to teach the twelfth-grade course on the development of animals and of the human being and how to take care of babies, and so forth, to a large class. Before I entered the classroom one tall boy came up to me, saying, "Mrs. Glöckler, don't think you can tell us that the human being does not come genetically from the monkey." Of course I *did* want to tell them this—it was terrible. And I thought: Now it's impossible to show them these pictures, I can't speak about the monkeys to this age group. So I spoke about the other vertebrates more and showed them this picture and simply asked them: What do you see? What is the developmental progression? And they realized that it is definitely the other way around, and they were so impressed. We then had a very good discussion about Darwinism and questions of development, of how body and spirit are related.

We can see that, with respect to form, spiritually the human being simulates the animals' development but that physically the animals move away from the human form and go into their animal specializations. With the human being we have the opposite: physically we have the human form, but spiritually we carry the animal kingdom in us, in our emotions, in our aggression. Spiritually we suffer from unconquered animal-likeness. Similarly, we have the life of the plants in us; it becomes apparent when we fall ill that we must continually overcome this kingdom too. And the mineral kingdom, too. If the mineral kingdom is too prominent in us, then we have all those illnesses of bone and deposits. So we see that in the human being the human form materializes physically but spiritually we always have to overcome the other kingdoms. It is very important for teachers to understand this huge tension which is always present in the body's growing processes.

The upright position of the human skeleton is unique in the animal kingdom. This form looks very like a large newborn, just grown bigger. It is unspecialized, and it is due to this lack of specialization in form that we have what amounts to a great surplus of the etheric growth forces which in the animal go into physical specialization. In the human being these forces remain and transform into soul and spiritual activity. The secret of human development is that we are able by nature to transform the forces of growth activity from the physical sphere into a spiritual growth process. Therefore, as those of you who have parent evenings know, we love to show the children's drawings. There one can see how this wonderful surplus activity, this etheric constructive power which is released from the body can be grasped, can give the hands and even sometimes the feet an impulse to be active, to be productive, to do something constructive.

And when children paint, they start first to paint their own constitution. You can see very wonderfully here how a three- or four-year-old child is able to paint its international archetypal form. All over the world children draw the same drawings. They even start to draw their own rhythmical system, as we know from books about children's drawings. It is good to realize how concrete this is and that artistic processes are nothing else than using the surplus growth activity which is no longer needed for tasks in the physical realm. We teachers are the transformers of natural forces into cultural forces of art and spiritual activity.

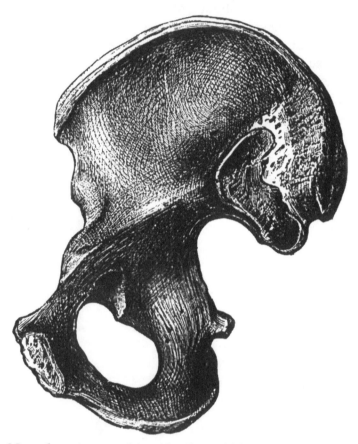

Now there is something else I would like to add. This is the bone of our hip. This structure is the pelvis; this is the part on which you are sitting now. In the upright position of the skeleton, we have a wonderful lemniscate form. I will only show this one picture, but you can also find this lemniscate structure in many places in the body, in the heart, in the muscles, in the knee. The lemniscate always appears where the function is to balance polarities. Here in the hip we have to balance the body weight between back and forth, right and left, and up and down. It is the most powerful region for balancing all the different forces of the body weight in all the directions of space. This form has the maximum geometrical capacity for balancing all the different sorts of polarities. It is the archetype for a rhythmic form which is able to bring into equilibrium all exaggerations of different positions. This is just one example of how economically the body works and how every form really speaks about its function.

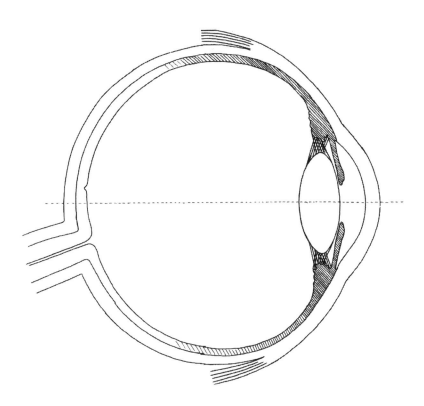

Another example is the form of the eye: the wonderful clear hole, the nerve part of vision, the lens, the iris, and the pupil where light and color can come in. We see it is constructed so that the specific function of looking is revealed. It even has a round, global form to suggest that it can make global pictures of the entire cosmos, the whole world. Such images help us to understand the forces with which the teacher is working in education, and how to support and nurture the physical growth processes.

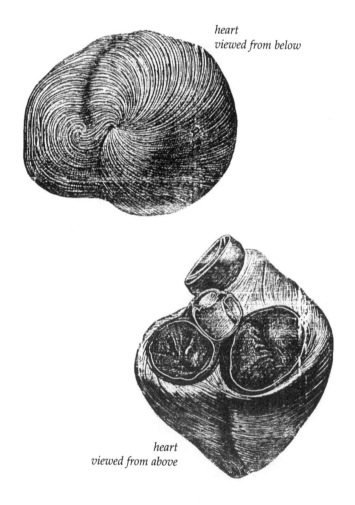

heart
viewed from below

heart
viewed from above

The function of the heart is, on the one hand, to suck the blood in during the relaxation phase of the heart muscle (diastole), when the fully relaxed muscle of the heart gives space to the entering blood. And in the contraction (systole), blood is pushed out. So we have this double function of sucking in and pressing out, and this is exactly what we see in the form of the heart looking from above.

The whole physical body speaks a language; everything in the human being speaks about its function. We can take all the details and we can take the whole; it is always the same. We rightly speak of the image of the human being which reveals what it is. I already mentioned earlier that we carry our whole body in uprightness. What does the language of the body say through this upright posture? Our very body says that we are upright beings. We can take this both in the literal, spatial sense, and also in a spiritual sense in that "upright" is another word for truthful, to be upright. So our body's language speaks about our spiritual function, that both outwardly and inwardly we are upright beings. Due to this uprightness we have a center between above and below, and this center is the seat of the force of the heart, of love. Love is the center of our upright being. The extreme polarities of our being are wisdom and power, but the most central force is love.

If we look at our hands from the aspect of the body's language, we can learn that we are disposed not be specialized, but what does this mean? We are free to take what we want and do what we want because our body does not dominate or force us into the direction of an adult (in the animal sense). You cannot tell by looking at my hand whether in the next moment it will take up a weapon in violence, or do something very soft. You can't see it. My hand's action depends on my invisible thought and emotion. I guide my body; my body does not guide me. We can see this disposition toward freedom because the anatomic structure of a hanging arm is only able to carry something—a suitcase, for instance. It is the anatomic disposition of the hand to carry a suitcase! For everything else I need to do something first to release my hand from its natural anatomic position. I need to bring it to a free place and then to do what I want with it.

As doctors and teachers we need to come to an understanding of what this delicate and extremely vulnerable human being is with its long physical development of about twenty years until the ego state is there. We must guide and help one another so that physical growth is stimulated in a way that allows the surplus forces to develop in a human direction and not in an animal direction. This is not easy, and therefore in our time we have worldwide problems in development. For example, there is the growing problem in the realm of attention deficit that we mentioned yesterday. In this situation it is difficult to reach the person's ego power and for the person to become aware and enter into constructive activity here and now. In this effort the head is the guide. People with ADD must learn to conceive an idea of what to do and command the attention necessary to fulfill a task carefully. I hope we will speak about such examples when we come to the more practical part of this conference. How can we give proper support so that the head forces can guide the learning process?

Then we have another huge problem, and that is the problem of addiction, in which the central forces of the heart, of love, are not sufficiently developed. In this situation there is no love for other people nor love for the world, no warm and light inner life. One needs the stimulation of physical substances to feel like a human being with an interesting inner life. In order to love other people better, to be less angry, to be less depressed, to have real interest in one another, we need the physical stimulation of drugs or medications. We wish to have an animal-like life in which our soul activity and our behavior is dictated by the organ functions and substance processes. Already twenty years ago, the World Health Organization published in a report that if addiction continued to grow at the same rate as it was growing twenty years ago, the worldwide situation in the year 2100 would be that every second person would be drug addicted, substance addicted. This problem has an exponential growth.

What does this mean for doctors and teachers? How must we guide and stimulate physical development so that the soul feels calm, full of light and color, in a sense satisfied in itself and ready to relate to the world and to people with compassion, love, and interest? What is the secret of our feeling life that it can so easily be squeezed between the above and the below until an emptiness occurs here, sucked out or pressed in, so that one needs help through taking medicines? It is a tremendous task first to understand this phenomenon in children and in adults and then to help to overcome this danger of straying farther and farther from proper human development.

Finally, after attention deficit and lack of love leading to drug addiction, we have a third problem, and this is the problem of aggression in the limbs and of sexual misuse and abuse. At the heart of this problem is an inability to use our physical body, our sexual and limb system, our metabolic and skeletal system, in a human way. The healthy human being guides and controls this system so that sexuality can be lived which is really human and not animal-like—although animals live their sexuality in natural rhythms. But if a human being is living with animal-like sexuality, it means that one is guided by one's physical drives rather than stimulating one's own drives in the direction in which one wants them to go.

These are the main problems of modern times. How can we educate toward a human use of sexuality and will activity and overcome crime and aggressive tendencies? How can we establish a healthy feeling life so that drug abuse is not the replacement for it? And how can we stimulate attention so that this upper part of the human being can be guided by the power of the ego? This is the big task we have to face.

I would like to conclude this introduction to the delicacy of the growing process and its proper stimulation with a physiological picture that may be familiar to many of you. From this chart we can see how the growing process between birth and twenty years progresses for different organs. The hundred percent line represents the adult level. The thymus gland

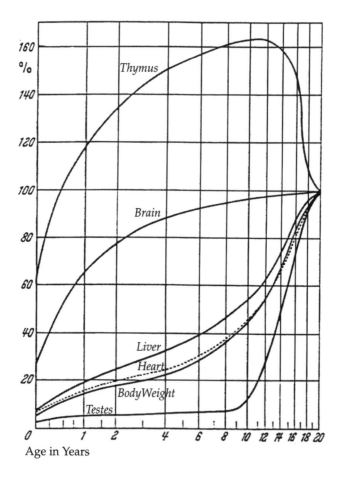

Age in Years

develops rapidly up to the tenth or eleventh year followed by a decrease down to the adult level. Then we have a very interesting process in the growth of the sexual organs whose growth curve is opposite to that of the thymus and brain.

Recall the picture I showed you of the huge head organization of the embryo. We see from that how in early childhood there is a maximum of brain growth that continues after birth for the first two years of life. Eighty percent of brain development occurs in those first two years, and that's the time in which children learn so very much, including language. When children enter kindergarten at three or four years of age, almost ninety percent of their brain development has already taken place. So the most delicate period in which we can fail the most are the first three years, because the faster a physical structure grows the more vulnerable it is. In kindergarten between the ages of four and six, something is still going on, but throughout the later school years the rate of growth continues to decrease. So a teacher in the upper grades has less chance of unwittingly doing harm than the kindergarten teacher has. For this reason Rudolf Steiner didn't allow certain people to deal with small children. For example, he told E. L.— who was a very good mathematician and physicist—to start in the upper school. He said, "You must first take high school students for some years and then we will think about giving you a first grade class." Things have changed very much, but Steiner thought completely physiologically, and he knew how great the impact of one person on another is through the pedagogical law I introduced yesterday. Therefore, he said, in the high school you can't affect the child's constitution anymore; but here in the early years there is a lot happening and therefore kindergarten teachers should be older, riper, maturer. Well, we can't do everything the way it should be done, but it's very good to know something of the ideal, for it strengthens us just to know that the smaller the child is, the greater our influence is on its constitution.

In the development of the function of the sexual organs, ovaries and testes, we have the inverse curve of that for the brain. Throughout the first six years there is almost no development, and then in pre-puberty beginning with the eighth or ninth year, things start to happen. Growth becomes rapid with the tenth year, and then it goes up between ten and sixteen to almost ninety percent of the function. You can see that that's absolutely the inverse situation of the brain development. This is really the signature: first comes the brain, and then the sexual organs. This gives a certain biological guideline; first we need to be well-established in the thinking so as not to come into misuse of the other part of the body, which therefore develops later. If we want to prevent problems in the sexual region, then it is important to work to establish our head well and the whole guidance of the nervous system. In this way, when sexuality develops, there is already an established guide.

We can now understand why Rudolf Steiner so often brings into his pedagogical lectures the fact that there are two different growing impulses in the child. The first growing impulse comes from the etheric. This is a modeling, structuring impulse beginning with the large head, this wonderful brain curve. Already in the first seven to eight years, most is established, and this growing period is quite harmonious. Then there is an opposite growth push in the adolescent, starting from below with the sexual functions and with hands and feet. The astral forces guide this second push. These forces do not sculpt but rather have a musical quality. Tomorrow I will speak of the impact of the musical astral forces and of the speech forces on the growing process, and then we will go into the pedagogical consequences of drama.

Lecture 3: The Metamorphosis of Growth Forces into Intellectual Forces and the Rhythmic Nature of Astral Activity

Tuesday, February 17, 1998

The growth activity of our body is silent. It is so silent that we have to give ourselves a certain push to realize that at every moment there is a growing and building-up activity in children's bodies.

I would like to show you one of the wonderful dynamics of the growing process, the growth of body weight in relation to body length. We know the typical growth from all the notes mothers keep when they have a baby and the doctor measures the baby's weight and length and looks at her charts to see what percentile of growth the child is in. Is it normal, premature, or exaggerated in one area or another?

The dynamic of growth is slightly different in girls and in boys. It is difficult to see the special dynamic in this growing process that we teachers and doctors are companions of. I will now give some specific examples so that this dynamic can speak more clearly to us.

Boys are heavier at birth; girls gain a bit faster and are about the same weight by age 4. By age 12, boys' weight is increasing at a faster rate. The girls' rate of gain slows markedly at around 15 while boys continue to gain at a fast pace til 18 and beyond.

40

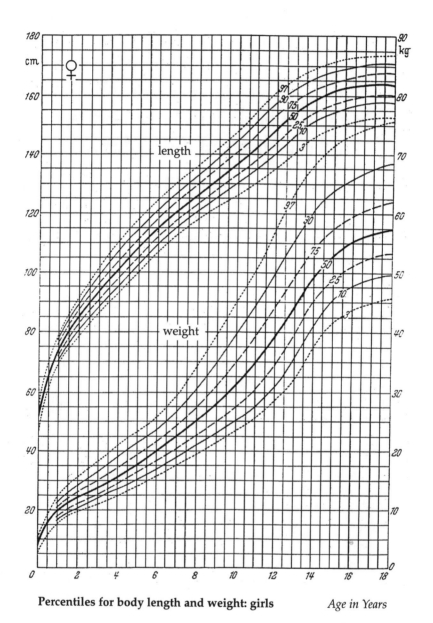

Percentiles for body length and weight: girls   *Age in Years*

With respect to length, boys are also longer at birth. However, girls increase more rapidly in length/height, becoming taller than boys by age 10. The boys then grow faster,

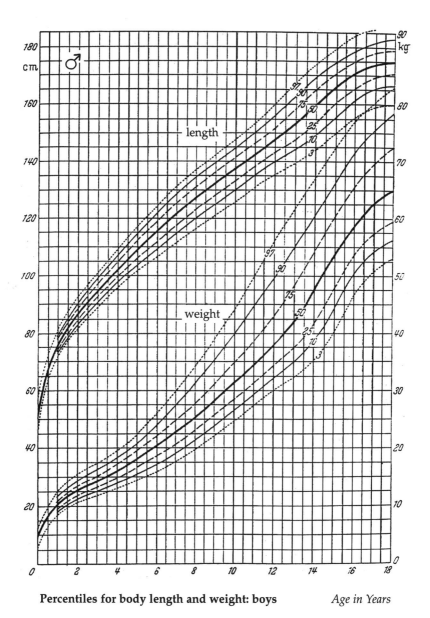

Percentiles for body length and weight: boys   *Age in Years*

becoming taller than girls by about age 16 when girls' rate of gain levels off. Boys then continue to grow taller til about age 18.

Yesterday we saw that the embryo was less than two centimeters long after two months. So, astonishingly, the embryo grows three kilos and fifty centimeters in the last seven to eight months of pregnancy. In the beginning, the progress of weight and length is very slow, but during those same first two months of intrauterine development there is a tremendous act of formation. The complete foundation and constitutional imprint of all the body forms is laid then, and the rest is just increasing weight and size. The physiognomy is already formed and ready during these first two months when weight and length play almost no role. Thus there is a certain tension between form and substance. At the beginning of pregnancy we can measure much form and very little substance, while at the end of pregnancy we can measure less form and more substance.

At birth the baby weighs three kilos and is half a meter long. Then in the first seven-year period, the body gains twenty more kilos. At five months a baby weighs six kilos—it has doubled its birth weight. This is of course the only time in the human life that we can double our weight in five months. Later on we would never succeed even if we tried. We could not even calculate how heavy we would be if we continued to grow at this rate—but of course we don't. In the first seven years we gain a total of about twenty kilos, in the next fourteen years almost another twenty kilos.

It is interesting that approaching age fourteen, from ten on, we have first a differentiation between male and female and then again a balancing process. In the last seven-year period nearly the opposite is the case. Boys gain another twenty-six kilos on average, while girls gain a mere eleven. So the dynamic is that girls have the experience of becoming heavy before and during puberty, and boys feel the high point of getting heavy later, at about sixteen or seventeen.

There is a similar dynamic regarding length. Between birth and seven years, body length increases by an average of seventy-eight centimeters from the birth length of fifty centimeters. At seven the average length for both sexes is one meter and twenty-eight centimeters. Then during the second seven-year period, boys grow an average of twenty-eight centimeters, while girls again grow faster, averaging thirty-one centimeters. And then in the third seven-year period, boys grow an average of twenty centimeters, while girls gain only six.

So the vertical process of growing longer or taller, and the horizontal process of gaining weight, are very different. Horizontal growth proceeds very evenly in harmonious steps of twenty kilos, on average, per seven-year period. By contrast, vertical growth begins with the largest percentage happening during the first seven years. Then in the second period there is less than half the first period's growth. And then in the third period, both sexes together average about a third, although for women there is only a little bit of growth in the third period. So the greatest increase is about a hundred percent, then about fifty percent, and then about a third.

So we can begin to understand that the first seven-year period is the time in which the etheric body, the carrier of our growing forces, is the most active. Then this tremendous growing activity must diminish, and this is what we call "school readiness." This transition includes the change of teeth and the metamorphosis of growth forces into intellectual forces. At this time a major portion of the etheric forces which were stimulating the prolific growth activity in the first seven years, is liberated from the body. Only about half of the etheric forces remain in the physical body to proceed more slowly and carefully with the body's further growing process. And then at the end of the second seven-year period, there remains in the physical body only a third or less of the etheric forces, depending on how many centimeters one still has to grow after puberty to reach one's full height. So this diagram makes clear that the vertical growing process is very special and has distinct qualities in each of the seven-year periods.

I would now like to go into a brief description of how the astral and ego forces participate in this growing activity and how the qualities of the etheric, astral, and ego forces work together and transform bodily activity into soul and spiritual activity. We have these qualities that we call etheric forces, astral forces, and the forces of the ego organization, and the question is: How can we gain a concrete perception or concept of these forces? Yesterday I tried to give an overview of the building up process of the physical body. We compared human and animal growth processes and arrived at the image of specialized animal growth and unspecialized human growth. This is the key image we need in order to understand the metamorphosis of the etheric forces from physical activity into thinking activity. In animals the etheric forces work entirely within the physical body with none remaining, and the result is one hundred percent intelligence in the physical body. This is the enormous wisdom and intelligence in the physical instinctual programming of all animals.

In the human physical body, however, we can observe that there is a great instinct deficiency. All the biologists of our century have discovered this and call it by different names. We all suffer from an instinct deficiency syndrome which makes it necessary for us human beings to learn things which the animals all know how to handle by nature. Animals know what to eat, how much to eat, and when to eat so that they remain healthy. Human beings have to learn this; we don't know it by nature. We have to devote a vast amount of intelligence to managing this eating problem, and very many people earn their money because people don't know this and don't succeed, and there are programs in schools for teaching the basics of health but with very little success.

I also mentioned the drug problem yesterday. Many of our illnesses come simply from our inability to sleep enough and at the right time. There are millions who use drugs just in order to sleep, and this is an increasing number. This instinct deficiency seems to grow. And after eating and sleeping problems comes sex. Of course it is the most natural thing for the sexes to come together so that new animals and human beings can be born. And the animals know exactly how to do this in a good fashion, but human beings have a great deal of trouble with it. All the newspapers are full of this: how to do it. And even the president sometimes has trouble with it. This instinct deficiency is general, is global.

But this seemingly problematic need to balance our instinct deficiency with intelligence is actually the basis of our dignity as human beings. Freedom as a quality, as a dimension of soul and spiritual development, needs this lack of instinct as its physiological foundation. Instinct is a wisdom which does not leave us free. If the instinct program is very well constituted, we will always follow it. Then on this level we don't think, we just act. So the more deficiencies we have, the more freedom we can develop. We can teach our body how to form its habits, how to react, how to act, and therefore we need a lifelong program of education just to train our freedom and to balance out our instinct deficiency. The clearer we understand this problem the clearer and more concretely we can understand the nature of the etheric forces.

Rudolf Steiner suggests that we observe the metamorphosis of growing forces into intellectual forces. I first began studying and observing this when I worked as a school doctor, visiting in the first grade. And I knew that a great change takes place in the etheric forces between the ages of six and eight, and I knew that this has something to do with teeth. The hardening process of the substance of the second teeth takes place between six and eight, and the average is seven. The second teeth actually come in over the course of seven, eight, or nine years, but the maturation of the substance itself, of the enamel, occurs at age seven.

And if it is true that we think with the same forces with which our body forms and grows, then we must see the biting quality in the intellectual activity of the first and second graders. Everything you find in the growing activity of your body you can also find in your thoughts. I'll give some examples to make it obvious and leave it to you to work out all the bits in between.

If you observe a first grade and the teacher says to the children, "Now I will tell you the story of such-and-such, and some of the children already know it, then you will likely witness different reactions from the children. Among the first graders who know the story already, you will find two groups: one group gets a wonderful gleam in the eyes suggesting, "Ah now I get to hear this story once more," and they are happy to listen. In these children the maturation of this part of the teeth is not yet complete. They are still in the kindergarten state and have a memory which loves repetition, which experiences itself as memory through repeating something. And then you have the children who react, "Ugh, I already know that one, can't you tell us something interesting, something new?" These children have already transformed their etheric forces from the teeth. They can bite something spiritually. This is the basis of abstract memory. Those who have an intellectual bite can hold a story, hold a content, hold on to something they have learned. They want to go a step further, to repeat only if they have missed or forgotten something or to get it clearer, but not because it's so nice.

It was wonderful for me to realize how obvious this is, because I have often asked myself: Why always these teeth? What is unique with these teeth, why is it so important? We have so many interesting organs, why always these teeth? But then I realized that this is the one and only organ that has no regeneration—therefore all the dentists live on it—absolutely no regeneration. Our nerve system regenerates wonderfully during the night, but during the day this system has no possibility for new cell growth. So the nerve system is the next most important system for thinking activity. And those organs which have a great turnover of cell regeneration and creation are at the third level. But the teeth have liberated one hundred percent of their etheric forces for thinking activity, and that's the only organ which can do so. All the other organs can only metamorphose those etheric forces that are not used for regeneration.

We have already seen that in the beginning of pregnancy there is the most forming activity and the smallest increase of weight and length. Similarly, in the first seven-year period there is most importantly a pronounced activity of forming and growing. This is followed by a dramatic reduction of this activity. The forming forces must leave the body, so all the sense organs, the brain organ, the whole nervous system, stop their forming activity after eight and nine years. The eye organization and the ear organization are completely mature by this time. Indeed, all the sense organs can only be stimulated to form better during the first seven years. The next group—the rhythmic function, the heart and lungs—takes longer, about sixteen years—girls a bit earlier, boys a bit later. And the metabolic system and skeletal system take from eighteen to twenty-one years to be completely worked out.

At the time of entering school, between age seven and eight, our nerve and sense organ systems release the greatest portion of forming activity into the developing thinking capacity. In first- and second-graders, we can observe the picture quality of thinking, the forming activity of thinking. The thinking faculty in a child of this age does not yet have the dynamic of the organ function of our rhythmic system, the rhythm of breathing in and breathing out, and the beating of the heart. Neither do children in the early grades yet have something which only the high school students have, and that is the quality in their thinking which comes from the skeleton and metabolic system. This quality is one of reproduction and creativity. This quality in the thinking begins with puberty when we become reproductive physically, and as our metabolic system takes some years to fully mature, so this capacity in our thinking develops over time.

It is important for us as doctors and teachers to look at the development of thinking activity with regard to the physical body, because we must always remember that the intellectual activity that I teach the students must correspond to their age. When the most formative activity of the etheric forces is liberated from its task of forming the nervous system and the sense organs, we gain the capacity to build something up in pictures and to memorize pictures. This is why children are so attracted by everything that is picture-like and moving, because this is the dynamic of the etheric forces.

At fourteen, new qualities are introduced when the etheric forces, which were working through the rhythmic system, are liberated from the body and combine with the astral forces, which are also freed at age fourteen. The new etheric quality enters the thinking capacity, and the liberation or birth of the astral forces provides the foundation of our mature emotional life. Before the birth of the astral forces, the emotional life is linked with the physical body, while afterward the emotional life becomes connected to the conscious life. We no longer react physically in emotional states as children do; for instance, when children are joyful, they jump. No adolescent would jump when he has joy. With adolescence, as these forces are liberated from the body, emotions can increasingly be handled purely as soul activity, related less and less with the physical. We then have the task of involving the liberated feeling life with the intellectual activity of this age. This is one of the most delicate pedagogical problems, and we must come back to it later.

But first I would like to complete this overview of the metamorphosis from body-forming activities into soul and spiritual faculties by finishing this section on the intellectual forces and then by describing the freeing process of the astral forces and the ego organization forces, because naturally we work with all three together. I will try to be as brief as possible in building a common foundation for our further steps on working in a medical pedagogical way.

Let us look once more at the fact that we work with etheric forces in the realm of thinking. The functioning of the different organ systems in the body is highly varied, detailed, and exact. Let us reflect for a moment on our thinking, and experience how we also have in our thinking a completely functioning organism with all the details in it that our physical body has. I have given one example for teeth, but let us now examine further how our thinking activity works.

We find growing activity in our thinking, of course. Our wisdom, our thoughts, our visions, our views can grow. We also find the whole process of digestion in our thinking. Our physical metabolic system, which has the capacity for analytic and synthetic processes, matures between the age of fourteen and twenty-one, so in teenagers we begin to find this quality-manifesting as a capacity for philosophical thinking, for analytic and synthetic thought processes. When we digest, we engage in an analytical activity, even if we digest our body's own substance. We see it in the death and regeneration of cells. And in the reconstruction of the body's own substance we have the process of synthesis in a most wonderful and complex form. So we have the possibility of thinking analytically and critically, pulling everything to pieces, because in our thinking we are using our forces of digestion. The same force which builds up the digestive tract gives us the power of our spiritual digestion.

We can go on, organ by organ. We can also look at the presence of the four elements in our physical body and in our thinking. There is solid form and substance in our bones and liquid substance in our blood and intercellular liquid. Air penetrates everything, oxygen transported by blood breathes in and out, and there is air in our digestive tract, in the stomach. We have airy structures, and we have warmth. And of course we carry these four qualities in our thoughts.

We have thoughts which are specifically formed like solid substances, and this is the whole area of our mental pictures. Today you can reproduce exactly the pictures I showed yesterday, for you have the capacity to adapt your etheric forces to the solid, physical facts and can keep them in your memory exactly. This is the activity of the etheric when it forms certain structures in physical substance.

Then there is the quality of the etheric forces which keeps everything liquid, which never allows liquid processes to come to a specific form. This is the quality your thoughts have when you produce concepts, for example, when you know what a lamp is—not this specific one which you have a mental picture of, but the principle, *lamp*, out of which you can construct a million different lamps. In this quality of thinking, you have in mind the significance, the spiritual concept of a thing, its definition, without having a specific mental picture. It is important to gain an impression of how varied our thinking activities are. We can fix our thoughts into certain solid pictures and thereby imitate physical structures. We can also leave the physical structure open and can experience thought in its forming character without reaching a form. We do this when we work with mathematical terms. For instance, the definition of a circle as "a plane curve everywhere equidistant from a certain point, the center" is not a picture of a certain circle. It is a pure idea which has the living power to construct a mental picture but which has the quality of holding back before it is constructed to leave it open to construct many other forms. This is pictureless thought. But in our time in which we learn in school and through TV only to think in pictures, people often do not realize that they also have this pictureless thinking, the capacity for pure philosophical thought, thinking without pictures.

Then there is a third dynamic in thinking, the air function which we call the getting of an idea. Ideas come and go. If for example a very good idea suddenly comes to you, you don't ask yourself where it comes from—you are just happy that it comes. This is the light of an idea. If we don't bite it, then it will go away again, and then we will say, "Oh I had such a good idea, but it's gone." Here we experience how our thinking organism is not a closed system but is a neutral, open, breathing system. It has as its dynamic the airy activity of breathing in and out.

And we have as the fourth quality of warmth in our thoughts the great burning activity which we can discover when we experience the spiritual warmth connected with finding our life ideal. This life ideal is something we can make many pictures of. We can have ideals about our life ideal, we can have concepts, we can think it without pictures, we can feel it as a power, and we can make very concrete mental pictures of it. The ideal reaches and penetrates every function of our thinking organism. It is something like the heart—it is the warmth center of our thought. We subordinate everything to our life ideal, we serve it with our whole spiritual activity.

And so if we look at the whole function of our organism, taking seriously this guideline of the metamorphosis of body-forming etheric forces into intellectual forces, then we see that this is the creativity with which we can balance our instinct deficiency. Of course it is important that we develop this keen fourfold intelligence so that the ego learns body-free, living thinking. And if this can't be learned and the awakening of the human being in the spirit does not take place, then the person remains addicted like a small child to his body forces and activities and cannot realize his spiritual birth. From this we come to all the forms of addiction, of needing permanent stimulation for spiritual activity through drugs. Therefore it is a huge endeavor, a greater task than it was fifty years ago, that we help children to work through their whole thinking organism so that they can experience their own spiritual being in thoughts and can break through to a pure spiritual activity.

This is the one area, the transformation of etheric forces into spiritual activity and the awakening of the ego in one's spiritual body. We will now move on to look at the next area, the level of the astral forces. Some of the questions you gave me Sunday and Monday concern how we can understand our middle region. I had said that love has to do with this middle part, wisdom with the head, and will with the skeletal and metabolic systems. Some of you then said that it's clear that the brain and sense organs are the physical carriers of our intelligence, and of course physical strength and activity depend on the metabolic system, but how can we understand physiologically that love is centered in the rhythmic function of heart and lung?

Here we enter into the realm of emotions as such, and love is the most central feeling, the most central emotion we have. Now what is the difference between the growing forces of the etheric, the forming, picturing, and thinking forces, and the astral forces of feeling? The emotional life follows completely different laws from those of the thinking activity. It is an entirely different realm of self-experience, although of course there is interrelationship. If we isolate these astral forces to look at them, we discover tension and relaxation. I can measure every tension and relaxation in numbers, and I can even describe the rhythm between tension and relaxation with certain rhythms. Our whole life of emotion can be characterized by rhythms, by tension and relaxation. We all know love is wonderful, and we want to have it every day. This is not at all like the story of the first-graders' "Oh, I know that story, now I would like to have something different." Impossible. If we look at our emotional life, we are even addicted to certain emotions, and if we don't get them or cannot activate them by ourselves, then we take a drug to have them. We are dependent on repeating emotions again and again because the feeling life is a rhythmic life and not an abstract intellectual life. Emotions can grow and differentiate, but they will repeat and repeat and repeat throughout our whole life. A baby is able to feel joy and pain. We have these feelings throughout our life, and even on the last day of our life we can still feel joy and pain.

If we compare this with our thinking activity, with our spiritual growing and changing, just think how often we change our minds—I hope. We do not repeat and repeat and repeat what we already know with no change. If we do, that's mental illness. In the emotional life, however, feelings give us a certain continuity, and love is the basis of a healthy emotional life. It can grow, but there is no change. In the growing process feelings become purer, clearer, and more intense, but they will always keep their quality. The essence of fear, of love, of devotion is always the same.

Therefore I have difficulty concentrating while you are singing in the mornings. I love music so much and especially the purification process of the artistic activity whereby it becomes better with every repetition. It is wonderful just to listen to this clearing and intensifying process that comes with practice. And every sound is a certain frequency, a certain tension (this is most obvious when one plays the notes on a string), and there is a certain rhythm. We can immediately see the influence of music and rhythm on our own rhythmic system. For example, if you listen to a good classical concert, you will notice that a symphony, for example, has different parts to it, each with its own character. There might be a quick part, a very slow one, then something in between, and then a powerful choleric finale. In these classic parts of a symphony you often find an adaptation of human temperaments: the minuet is sanguine, the finale quite often choleric, then you have a very phlegmatic slow section in between, and usually a large, heavy, rather melancholic introduction. It is very interesting to see how music is adapted to the basic emotional qualities of the human being. And if you observe the rhythm of your breathing and heartbeat, you will see a synchronization going on during the concert. The rhythm of your breath and of your heartbeat changes in the slow and the quick parts of the symphony. Our heart has its tone, has its rhythm, is itself an instrument. And the breath provides the beat for the quicker melody of the heart.

We don't think about this usually, but if we look at formative activity from the point of view of the astral forces, then we can discover how many rhythms there are in our body, rhythms which are pure expressions of the astral forces which bring numbers—beat, rhythm, and repetition—into the whole body function. This rhythmic capacity is the basis of the emotional life and frees itself from the body at the age of fourteen. As the emotional life becomes more and more free from the body functions, we become able to enter with our feelings into the realm of the spirit, to feel, for example, the beauty of a thought. Of course our astral forces always remain partly in the body, like the etheric forces, but we can liberate our emotional life to a greater or lesser degree from the body functions.

54

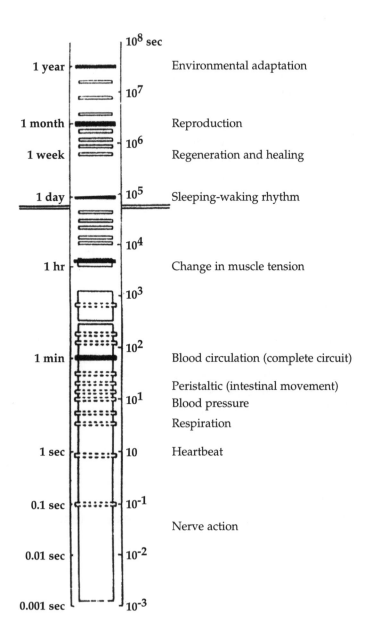

Duration of rhythms

And now I would like to give a brief overview of the wonderful way in which our body is penetrated through and through with astral rhythmic activity. We have periods of parts of seconds in our nervous system, in the polarization and repolarization processes on the membranes of our nerve cells, a rhythm of very high frequency. Then we have periods of seconds in the rhythmic activity of our heartbeat. The rhythms of our breathing activity have periods of between seconds and minutes. Then there are rhythms that take hours in the vegetative system, for example the rhythms of contraction and relaxation in the metabolic tract of our stomach and intestines. The rhythm in this process is very slow, but the power with which it tenses and relaxes changes in rhythms of an hour. Then we have the sleeping-waking rhythm and the daily, or circadian rhythms.

Then come weekly rhythms, and this includes the wonderful regeneration rhythm. For example, if you have a wound, it needs the weekly rhythm to heal. If it is a deep wound, in the first week there is a certain push to heal, and then in the second week you have another two- or three-day push of cell growth and then a pause, and after the seventh day another push. Or if you remove a kidney through an operation and only one kidney remains, then you have compensatory cell growth in the remaining kidney in a wonderful seven-day rhythm. That is the therapeutic reactive rhythm of the body. And four times seven days is the rhythm for longer recoveries. If one is really exhausted, one needs at least four weeks to recover. And if Waldorf teachers are worn out (kaput!), they are mostly so worn out that they need two or three times four weeks to really become who they were!

56

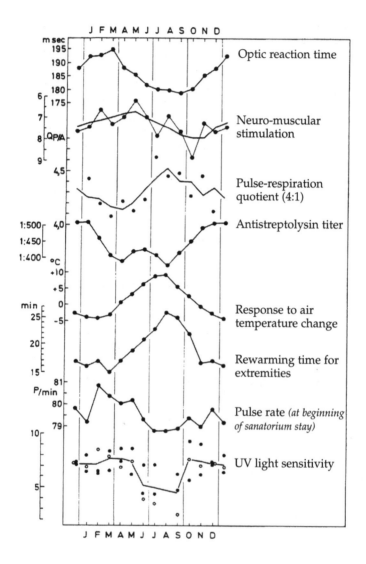

Then we have yearly rhythms, and I will show you some of the hundreds of details from chronobiological research which serve to illustrate this annual rhythm. The pulse, sensitivity to light, sensitivity to cold, antistreptolysin titer (a measurement for the status of an infection), even the way the pulse and the breath interact, these all have a characteristic yearly rhythmic curve. Very many functions change in the course of the year in a specific rhythm.

Number of reticulocytes in four groups of six healthy people
vacationing in higher altitude

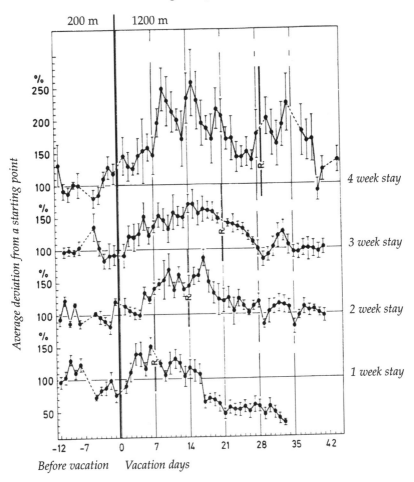

And here you see change in the blood's reticulocytes (particles responsible for clotting) in seven-day periods. If, for example, you go to a health resort and you go up to an elevation of 1500 meters in the mountains, your body will react in this classic seven-day rhythm, and your blood will build new blood cells, reticulocytes we call them, to adapt to the smaller amount of oxygen in the mountain air. This is a huge activity of regeneration and recovery of blood. And if you then come back down into the city again, your blood is refreshed.

58

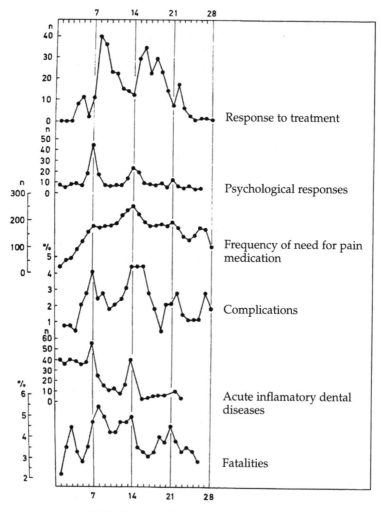

Critical points during a period of healing

And the same thing happens if, for example, you have had a heart attack and you go to a health center to recover for four weeks. The difficult times, the crisis points, are in a rhythm of seven days. You have the greatest number of fatalities in these periods if the regeneration is not successful. The critical turning points are the times before a new push of regeneration.

Then we see the same seven day periods with the interference of acute mental complications. The times at which people experience a need for analysis is rhythmic. A person calls one day saying, "I feel so bad." And when you look, it's this rhythm. People want the medicine for two days, then they say, "Oh that's better now." It is similar with how people are upon arrival at the hospital. For the first seven days they feel relaxed and fine, and after seven days they feel worse than they did at home. Then it becomes better, and at fourteen days they feel a little better than they had felt at home but still much worse than when they first came. And then you see a little peak in the third week, and then they always feel fine, and they can go home. So recovery patterns typically follow these seven-day periods.

Then we have the important daily rhythm of how our youngsters feel in school. They feel very good in the morning, and then all tired out between 1:00 and 2:30 when there is a sharp decline in their physiological activity. In the later afternoon there is a second peak when they are happy and like to be active, and then a second decline before the later evening when they want to sleep. So we also have to adapt, and this is a huge theme in itself, how to adapt the lessons of the day to the physiological rhythms of the child. Naturally, the best thing is to adapt the lessons to these activity peaks if possible.

And of course, knowing that the seven-day rhythm is the rhythm of the body's health reaction, we can see that the five-day school week does not support the healthy activity of the body. In Europe we have done research which shows that students in schools which have a five-day rhythm are ill more days each year than students who are in schools which have a six-day rhythm. But this is not astonishing, for it stems from the physiological capacity of the organism. If you have a five-day program, then you have two simultaneous rhythms which work a bit against each other. You have five days, and then the beginning, one, two, of the next rhythm. And then that's broken and you have one, two, three, four, five, it's broken; and one, two, it's broken. Whereas the rhythm of seven adapts these forces and brings the etheric and the astral into a harmonious relationship. All these numbers come from the astral. Numbers are music. They provide the tension and the foundation of every relationship, for between numbers there are certain relationships. The astral body is the body of relationships, of numbers, of proportion, of what we can count, the source of the qualities which bring the individual imprint of the rhythmic system into the etheric. The rhythmic system plays between the etheric and the astral, but the quality of the imprint of each number and the ratios comes from the astral. We take care of the emotional life of children by maintaining good rhythms in everything we do.

Lecture 4: The Ego Organization as the Great Integrator

Wednesday, February 18, 1998

Good morning, dear friends. This morning I would like to finish the medical or physiological foundation aspects of Waldorf education, and I hope that it's possible in the last part of the morning to go into some of the questions I have received from you.

On Sunday we started by looking at some of the basic concerns of our time and asking the question: What is an adequate education for tomorrow? What faculties, forces, or possibilities must the human being have in order to face the near future, to be ready for life, to be able to stand and to digest what time brings and not to break down under all the information and attacks of modern times? What does the human being need in order not to look for a happy fantasy land in which concrete development cannot take place, but only fun and living for oneself? And on Sunday evening we also looked briefly at the pedagogical law. I hope that we can come back to this tomorrow from the more practical point of view of how to work with it in school to meet the problems we have. Then I started to widen our understanding of the sheaths, the four members of the human being, through physiological study. Many questions have arisen in response to this, and in my concluding remarks this morning I hope to help you to understand the correspondence between the different aspects better.

Yesterday we began by focusing on the etheric body and its transformation into the formative, creative capacity of thinking. Then I gave a brief description of the astral forces as forces of music. When you make music, as you did just now, you can experience that you are dealing with numbers, not only that every tone is a single little number—first, second, third tone which then creates a melody—but you also have to count: daa daa daa daa, da-da-da-da-daa. You are lost without numbers in music, it's impossible. You need numbers to have rhythms, you need numbers to find a certain harmony and to find in harmony a certain proportion or relation between the notes, and you even need numbers for the melody which has a first and a last note. Our musical memory also works with numbers: we know that one phrase, d-d-d-d-d, is still missing; what was it? And you remember the phrase more easily if you know how many tones it was or how the rhythm went. Numbers serve music, proportions serve music, and the relation between the numbers, between or in the proportions, serves or expresses music. And the phenomenon of tension and relaxation that we have in music is the basis for every feeling experience or emotion we have. Even if we are relaxed and feel very calm and peaceful, there is still a certain basic tension in this, a relaxed tension.

So that was yesterday, how the astral forces structure the body so that we can count our fingers, so that we have proportions throughout the body. For example in our lung system there are three lobes on the right side and two on the left. And then our breathing in and out has this wonderful relationship between two and three which in music is the ratio of the interval of the fifth. I can fortunately refer you to Armin Husemann's book [*The Harmony of the Human Body: Musical Principles in Human Physiology.* Edinburgh: Floris Books, 1994] in which he has tried to work out from the basics how we are structured through music. I can only touch on it now.

We have yet to speak about the ego organization and its gifts to the body. The physical body brings nutrition and substance to our body, following its system of working laws. And there is an etheric system of working laws according to which the etheric body carries life and circulation and brings its sculptural activity. The astral forces bring proportion, structure, countable relationships, and numbers into the whole form of our body. The ego organization has still another system of laws. These do not deal with numbers, nor with producing forms as the etheric does, nor even with matter which brings every forming activity to death. The physical body is the master of death, of bringing things to an end, to a stop, bringing them out of life—frozen music, frozen proportion. Stop. End. When the physical dominates the rest of our being, then we die.

But the ego organization with its laws is something we can best describe as a system of laws which is able to integrate all the other laws, just as warmth has the capacity to dominate all other states. For example, if you have a piece of iron and heat it enough, it will become liquid. And if you put more fire and heat to it, then it will start to become airy. And if you bring an even greater intensity of fire to it, it transforms to the plasma configuration of matter in which you can no longer tell whether it is still matter or is pure energy. Warmth is the master magic working in matter, bringing it out of form, bringing it out of liquid, bringing it out of air, into this plasma state. And if you take away warmth, then matter becomes solid again. So the laws of warmth, of thermodynamics, are the only ones which really penetrate and dominate all the others. The state of matter in the physical body is also a result of the body's warmth activity. If there is too much warmth, then you have inflammation; if there is too little warmth, then you have deposits; and if there is just the amount of warmth so that everything gets the quantity of movement and flexibility it should have, then we are healthy. From the natural side we have warmth and its laws, and from the spiritual side we have the ego organization and its integrative capacity.

One of Rudolf Steiner's most wonderful discoveries is that the human being is not only constructed out of natural laws which we find in the solid, the liquid, the air, and warmth, but that the human being is also constructed through the laws of all the human arts. This is very basic and powerful. The art of architecture, for instance, comes from the physical body, from the surplus power of our structure. Of all the forms we have in buildings, there is not one which does not come archetypally from our bones and the forms of our organs—everything.

Roundness, the square—you can find the archetypes for all architectural forms in the body. We create body-related forms, and therefore we feel good in the buildings we have created.

Some of you may have had the experience of living, for example, in a flat in which the ceiling is two meters and twenty centimeters high and your body height is, for example, one meter eighty, so you can easily reach the ceiling with your hand. And if you are a bit disposed toward melancholy or depression, *you will become depressed.* You will get it very strongly and not know why. And a good psychologist or psychiatrist knows that if he is treating depression, he must ask about all circumstances, not only: Do you have any problems? but first of all: Where do you live? He must start with the simplest things, since our senses stimulate the physical body and affect the way our spiritual being feels in this body. If there is no space to breathe, if in form and color the architecture around us inhibits our feeling well, if there is a negative interaction and stimulation between the building around us and our physical body, then we feel unwell and dispirited. That is why in the Waldorf movement we take care, especially in kindergarten where it is most important, that everything speaks to the senses so that the proportions of the physical body are taken care of by the building and that all the senses are caressed, are loved by the impressions.

Architecture is the art of the laws of the physical body. As we saw earlier, sculpture is the art of the laws of the etheric body. Painting is the art in which the astral body projects its laws of proportion and numbers into the etheric field; then we have color tones, color moods, color proportions. The sculptural quality becomes penetrated with the laws of the astral and, if we want to help the interaction between the astral and the etheric, if we want to stimulate life forces by means of the astral, we need to paint and to form with colors. Then we also have music in which our *I* organization works in the astral.

Physical laws project into the surroundings in architecture. Etheric laws project into physical substance when we model with etheric activity in matter. If you engage in astral activity through the etheric body, then you have painting. And if you work with your inner *I* activity, your warmth, your will power, the essence of your being, into the astral, if you penetrate your astral body with your ego activity, then you have music. We feel at home in music, and we can become better human beings if we listen to, or if we ourselves produce, good music in which we can meet the *I*, our true spiritual being. In good music we meet ourselves in the realm of the astral. It is ego awareness in the astral. If we listen to good music, archetypally we experience: I live in my soul. Then we feel at home in our soul, satisfied, understood, balanced in the huge harmonies of the soul. In the end, good music brings us to a new balance in our soul. In this way music therapy can help the ego to find itself.

On the other hand, in our time we also experience the opposite. For if music takes the ego power not only into the soul but deeper, into the life body and physical body, then these laws penetrate too deeply. The rhythms and tones become too solid and physical and do not remain in the breathing of the soul. In this music, we leave aside our conscious ego and the higher emotions, and everything is only working in the hard beating rhythms in which we move our arms and legs [demonstration of hard rock dance movements, which play on the heaviness of the body]. In hard rock music, one loses one's *I* in matter. You can really see where these forces are drawn. As an experience, it is interesting—just to realize that this path is possible. But if one becomes addicted to it and only feels fine in losing oneself through the experience of this earthly physical music, then one loses the relationship to one's higher ego being. It is as if the *I* becomes drunk in the lower sheaths and loses contact with its true homeland.

Therefore it is tremendously important to educate musical understanding so that we gain a true experience of our identity between heaven and earth. If music lives and breathes in your soul, then you are between heaven and earth, you are in the middle, finding yourself as a being living between the worlds. But if you are one-sided at the extreme of the heavenly pole and have very melodious sounds not reaching the earth, or if you are at the other pole, living in the earthly music I just tried to describe, then the music loses its astral capacity to breathe between the worlds, and it imprisons the ego.

This is something we must look at very carefully in our time. For many children, the Waldorf school is the only place in which they can experience other qualities of music than they get at home, and it is important that they experience other qualities, even if it is only to the extent that they can remember later that there was something else. We know that the sphere of music can help us to deal with our aggressions, with our uncontrolled emotions, and that for many people music is a way to get rid of their untransformed, uncontrolled emotions. Shakespeare wrote this wonderful phrase in his drama *The Merchant of Venice:* "The man that hath no music in himself, nor is not moved with concord of sweet sounds, is fit for treason, stratagems, and spoils." And then he adds, "Let no such man be trusted" and that's the secret of music. If one has this music between heaven and earth in oneself, one is protected from— well, very simply, one is protected from the forces of hell.

But our ego doesn't only want to live in the astral, important though that is. The ego wants to develop higher faculties such as the Spirit Self. When the ego has lived in and transformed the astral body, that thoroughly purified astrality is the Spirit Self, a faculty which is beyond our ego. We gain it by transforming and purifying our astral body. In the Spirit Self, we are able to communicate with higher beings. Higher beings start to live in us just as we live in our lower members. We communicate through the Spirit Self with our thoughts, realizing more and more that thoughts and feelings are spiritual realities. We wake up to the reality of the spiritual world and find ourselves in the spirit. The law of this consciousness that we call Spirit Self already lives in all of us, and Rudolf Steiner describes this in the Curative Course when he gives the very first description of the pedagogical law: the laws of the Spirit Self work in the art of poetry, of speech. So now we come to the laws of Spirit Self active in the sphere of the *I*. That's poetry, that's *I*-culture.

There is something I have to add to the pedagogical law we spoke of earlier. We teachers educate from the higher to the lower [ego of the teacher influences the astral body of the child; astral body of the teacher affects the etheric of the child, etc.] and people were asking Rudolf Steiner: But who educates the ego? This applies particularly to curative education in which ego capacity, the control of thinking, feeling, and willing, is quite often not developed. Some people can't even speak or move properly. So who can educate this wonderful power of integration, of balancing? And Rudolf Steiner answered that this is the system of the laws of Spirit Self, and that you find these laws already working in language. The wisdom of language is transformed astrality. Speech is the astral quality completely dominated and worked through by the ego. If we speak consciously, we live in every word and sentence with our ego presence and our attention. Then we are able to hear what the language itself tells us; we are inspired by the reality, by the substance of words. Therefore there is no subject in the whole Waldorf curriculum, from kindergarten to twelfth grade, about which Rudolf Steiner gave so many indications as about speech and how to work with it.

To speak, to listen, to live with words, to do speech training, to learn to spell, to practice the consonants, the vowels, to go through all the revelations of language—religious language, meditative language, the language of prayer, poetical language, humorous language—we study and practice all types of language for two reasons. One reason is that speech is the most powerful activity for training a healthy breathing rhythm. We learn to breathe in a healthy way if we cultivate our language. We then breathe with enough oxygen, with enough depth in the breath so as not to hyperventilate. So on the one hand, physiological speech educates breathing. On the other hand, speech brings the wisdom of the Spirit Self into our ego awareness. Therefore meditation also starts with listening to words, to syllables like *aum*. We feel that the world of inspiration we enter through speech is a higher world, that speech is something like the last greetings in our normal life from this higher world.

Speech also protects us, for as long as we speak with one another, we don't become physically violent with one another. It protects and holds off aggression as long as possible. At first when people start to struggle with one another, you hear the beginning of it in the language. First people talk, and then a word comes in a tone which upsets the other person a bit. He feels attacked. And then we can have the level of verbal violence, and if one can keep the problem at this verbal level, it will of course be violent and aggressive, but only on the soul level, not breaking through to the physical level. Quite often, however, a moment comes in which we do not know what else to say. The other attacked us, and we want to give it back, and there are no more words; everything has already been said. And the point comes when, having no words anymore, we take something and throw it, or leave the room with a shout or with a remark. Then we are acting physically. This is a retreat back to the developmental stages of early childhood. We started with walking, followed by speaking, and finally thinking. If we stop thinking and only argue, that's the first step of regression, and if the arguments are exhausted, then the second step of regression comes and physical violence starts. This is the reason we have aggression in our culture. It is a lack of cultivation of speech. Nothing else. If people were able to speak about their problems, they would not have the need to be criminal. They could ask for something; they would have imagination and creativity; they could find a human solution for their problems. And therefore Steiner said criminality and aggression are merely a lack of education and specifically a modern speechlessness. And I must say, if students perform on stage, working with all these arts, it is an act of prevention for problems of this kind.

After Spirit Self we have a higher faculty, and this is the etheric body transformed by the ego activity into Life Spirit. And if this Life Spirit activity works through the Spirit Self, if the laws of the Life Spirit (which is nothing other than etheric laws dominated by the ego) are brought into the sphere of speech, of Spirit Self, and if this activity is then revealed through all the lower sheaths so that we can see it penetrating, then we have eurythmy. Eurythmy is the system of laws of the Life Spirit working in the realm of speech, of Spirit Self. And therefore, if eurythmy is really done and exercised, it is a very powerful and healthy art, for it brings ego control into this pure sphere of the etheric and then into physical revelation. This allows the laws of my higher self increasingly to dominate my physical, etheric, and astral constitution.

Eurythmy is an art which brings the physical and etheric bodies under the control of the ego, under the control of the spirit. Each movement helps the *I* to express itself in a meaningful way with respect to thought, emotion, and action. From the spiritual point of view, speech ability and peacemaking ability are a preparation for conscious experience of the Spirit Self. I hope very much that eurythmy will come to be discovered for what it is. It is not yet discovered; it is difficult to teach, I know that, but it is so difficult because it is so powerful. What I always love to say, and hope you will not misunderstand it, is that the most important thing for class teachers and kindergarten teachers, and even for high school teachers, is that they themselves develop a good relationship to eurythmy and speech because then their gestures, their movements, the way they can modulate their language, is so penetrated by the warmth and love of the ego sphere that when these people speak and act, the children are attracted to it. The more difficult the children are, the more the teacher must be spiritually present in finding the basis for discipline. From my experience discipline depends seventy percent on how you move and speak. If your speech is so magical for the children that they love to listen, and if your movements are attractive enough, then the children will feel stimulated to go into what you the teacher want. And a positive side effect of doing a lot of speech and eurythmy oneself is that one is able to do little exercises with the students. Or if one has to put something on the stage, one knows better how to move, how to act, and one becomes more flexible for this artistic activity. And if there is no eurythmy teacher at school, then you can do a little—but don't tell the eurythmists!

This is Rudolf Steiner's powerful discovery, that art has laws and that the laws of art are the forming activities of our own being, of our sheaths. Leonardo da Vinci also knew this but he did not yet have access to the anthroposophical study of the human being and therefore he formulated it differently. Leonardo da Vinci, the famous painter and architect, was brilliant in the arts, and he wrote a big volume for painters in which he said: The inexperienced artist doesn't know that he paints himself, that he always copies himself, because it is the soul who creates the body and the artist works with the same creative soul forces. The experienced artist knows this, and therefore he avoids it and creates objective things through his art, not projecting his own feelings and fantasies into it. Artistic training means learning not to unconsciously project one's own building, but to handle the formative forces of one's own body so objectively that one can reveal through them the facts of the world. And if one produces a self-portrait, then it is consciously done and not unconsciously projected.

So in artistic therapy, for diagnosis we let the children draw their own pictures or freely improvise music, because it reveals illness and health. It reveals the individual constitution. And therefore Rudolf Steiner did not want teachers to let children just paint freely in school. Rather we always give exercises or tasks so that the children learn to train their formative forces objectively, using healthy archetypes which bring health to the constitution, so that they do not project their illness but are injected with health. Children can receive health through a specific task for their formative forces. The artistic Waldorf curriculum has much to do with art therapy. It is a soft art therapy, an age-specific art therapy, and you the teacher are the therapist in this. And therefore artistic education is a very serious subject from the point of view of body formation and from the point of view of bringing health to the constitution for the whole life.

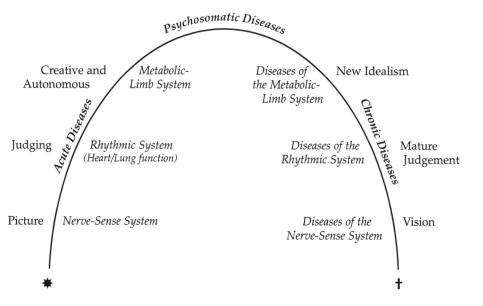

I would like to summarize these constitutional facts with a drawing. The line begins on the left in the growing period of the physical body and continues through the physiologically steady state between twenty and forty. (Most of you are still in this wonderful age. I've just left it, unfortunately. I'm here in the stage of decline.) The line then proceeds into the period of decline of our life forces when our capacity for regeneration decreases and we get old and weak. Finally the physical body gains total domination, the higher sheaths leave the body, and we are prepared for our spiritual birth and physical death. We have normal diseases which are characteristic for each period. Acute inflammatory diseases are typical for the building-up period of our body. These help to create a good immune system which can only be established if the body has to practice dealing with bacterial and viral diseases.

Then in the middle part of life we have to struggle with psychosomatic diseases, which are neither fish nor fowl. We don't know whether to get a prescription or rather to look for good advice on how to take our soul life into our own hands so that we do not project our soul problems onto the body. When we struggle with psychosomatic diseases, we can see especially clearly how the pedagogical law works. If we are unable to keep something in our astral body and work it through in our soul, then it goes one stage deeper and affects the functioning of our etheric body. And if we cannot cure it there by enough sleep and good habits, then it will break through into a physical illness.

Finally in the last third of life we have the disposition toward chronic diseases. It is interesting to look at how our body develops and how its involution takes place, all centered around the axis at midlife, a balance point in the middle of our biography.

By the age of eight or nine our nervous system and sense organs have developed, as we have seen. And when we ask ourselves what we can do to stimulate this development, then we have two magic words: attention and movement. Through attention we stimulate sense perception. If a child can't really look, if he or she has a tendency toward attention deficiency from the very beginning, then an adult needs to be with the child and help him to go into an observation by taking the child into his or her own attention, carrying the child in his or her own intentionality of looking or listening. This helps the child to feel secure, for if the body is calm then the intensity of looking and listening is helped.

The other magic word for the nerve system is movement, active, skillful movement. If we have, for example, a baby with oxygen problems at birth and a symptomatology of minimal brain dysfunction, what do we do? Gymnastics, curative gymnastics, movement. We need movement to cure and regenerate the brain. This is why it is so damaging for children not to move enough or skillfully enough, and for them not to create their own pictures and their own movements. If technology takes over the child's activity and the child is the great onlooker and the great controller, this is not at all stimulating for the nervous system and sense organs. This is a very big problem. We are already in the third generation of miseducation, and therefore we have children who bring these symptoms with them from the very beginning.

Of course there are always people saying that attention deficit is as old as mankind. Certainly. Most illnesses are companions of human beings. But in every period of history some illnesses are pushed to the top, and the attention deficit disorder has increased exponentially in my own lifetime. In Mexico City, for example, stimulated by pollution and by technological problems, it is already the case that thirty percent of all children suffer from this syndrome. Yet in 1960, when I lived in Mexico for one year, this disorder was completely unknown, and people were so nice in school, as they were in Sacramento thirty-seven years ago. It was a totally different scene.

We have the same phenomenon with drugs. Again, some point out that drugs are as old as mankind (sexuality also), that it's not an actual modern problem. I really must say, No. Of course drugs are as old as mankind, but the way mankind used drugs was very conscious. Whether for medical or for sacred, ritualized purposes, the use of drugs was maximally controlled and well integrated into the culture. What we experience now in the second half of this century is that people come into uncontrolled drug abuse and into a process of disintegration of culture, of creating subcultures. This is a totally new phenomenon. Even if one doesn't want to judge whether or not this drug subculture is the future of humankind, even if one leaves this open, one must say that it is a completely new problem.

The drug problem, the addiction to medications and drugs, is not the hard drugs. The drug problem is Prozac, the drug problem is amphetamines, the drug problem is Ritalin, the drug problem is that we are addicted to medications because we can't control our soul forces any more. The problem is that we can't live in our soul. The *I* feels unhappy in its soul and can't live there peacefully any more. The active struggling in the soul needs help from substances, needs a doctor. That's the problem, and that's new. In earlier times the single *I* was not emancipated. People were integrated in sex, rituals, and customs. If there was drug use, it was ritualized. They lived within social boundaries, in social forms which gave the individual a certain sense of well-being. Being drawn in by matter, by machines, by actions coming from outside, is something new, and it educates us to be passive and to become inwardly more and more empty. Often we can't stop this and so must find a balance for it. This is a big pedagogical task. We need to balance the dulling influence that our culture brings to bear on children with an education which—at least during school time—aids inner activity, soul activity, body activity.

In the period between age eight and fourteen or fifteen we have the physical development of the rhythmic functions. We need to stimulate these physical organs with all sorts of activity. Why? Because every artistic activity has something to do with rhythm. Every artistic activity must be practiced. One develops ability through repetition. One learns to repeat, to strengthen, to relax, to strengthen, to relax, to repeat, to repeat—that's breathing. On the one hand this helps to create such a rhythmic activity in the body and, on the other hand, our soul, our feelings, our emotional life, is most attracted by artistic activities. We always judge: Is it nice? is it not nice? can I have sympathy now, or do I hate that I have failed at the same thing three, four, five times, until I get angry? I would like to get it now! We are tremendously involved with our emotional life in the artistic activity, and therefore artistic activity helps to develop the rhythmic organs. Feelings deepen and activate the heartbeat and breathing process, as we mentioned yesterday.

Thirdly we come to the development of the metabolic system. One of the most wonderful questions in Waldorf education is how to stimulate the growth of the skeletal system and the activation of our metabolic system. Of course movement and artistic activity are good for everything, even for skeletal development because we use our physical skills, but they are not enough. There is actually no better stimulation for the growth and development of the skeletal and metabolic systems than having one's own good ideas.

For me the archetypical experience was a lesson in tenth grade. I was teaching the physiology of the heart, and I spoke about the circulation system and then asked the question: How did William Harvey discover that the circulation system is a closed system and not open, as Aristotle thought? I gave them the conditions, everything that Harvey used, and everything that Harvey knew out of the knowledge of his time, and I asked the children to be Harvey and to discover it now for themselves. Half an hour passed of real thinking and struggling and trying to become a little Harvey. Many suggestions were given of how we could find the secret to why the circulation is closed. Finally, after half an hour, one boy had the solution and found the same thought Harvey had found, and I said, "Wonderful! You are the Harvey of today. That's it."

And then I saw a miracle—for me it was really the eye-opener to this phenomenon. This boy completely changed his posture and the way he held himself. Before this he was not one of the best pupils, and he used to sit—tenth grade, remember—all slouched, like this [hanging over his desk, lying on his desk, lying back in his chair] to write (or not write) what I was saying. He always sat in the back of the room, and in this moment when the whole class faced him and was fascinated that this particular boy had found the solution, he sat fully upright. He looked out and was involved, and I saw then how the trust in one's own thoughts brings oneself into a new uprightness, into a completely different posture. The windows of my school doctor's room faced the school yard, and I saw this boy walking during the break, and he walked totally differently, like someone who has got something. It was so amazing to see him among those youngsters at break, pulling out their things and discussing, and now suddenly this new walk. You could really see how the ego organization, through the warmth of conscious thoughts, penetrated his body and brought it into a new position.

This is why the Parzival motif—question, question, question—helps the youngsters to find their own fitting ideas so that they can really become upright human beings. In this last seven-year period growth is dominated by the forces of the ego which is then born after one is completely grown up. During this time, increase in height and body weight is on average not so pronounced as it is during the astral and etheric growing phases, but in this last period the ego forces work through the body. We must stimulate the ego activity to work through the metabolic and skeletal systems by this awakening in thoughts and waking up to one's own upright stance. The way we teach helps tremendously in this stimulation of the physical development.

Then an interesting thing happens when we enter the last third of life. The system in which we first feel the decrease or the involution of our physical forces is the metabolic and limb system. Women begin to lose the capacity for reproduction between forty and fifty. Our skeletal problems usually start at that age, and incidents of rheumatism are typical. Then between fifty and sixty is the typical age for the onset of heart rhythmic disorder (first heart attack) and the onset of lung diseases like bronchitis. And still later we have the onset of chronic problems with the nervous system and sense organs. The organs which develop first have their involution last. The better an incarnation takes place through good stimulation, the less we have chronic disease problems in the last third of life. Therefore Waldorf education is really preventive care for the second half of life. This is a very important side effect.

On the chart you can also see the development of the intellectual forces, the thinking and picturing forces which we acquire when the etheric forces are freed from the nervous system. Then, when the rhythmic forces are freed for thinking, we gain the breathing activity in thinking which is judging: Shall I or shall I not? That's a rhythmic function in thoughts. And finally, we develop personal individual creativity, which is metabolic activity in thoughts. Producing one's own spiritual child and standing on one's own spiritual feet in independent thinking, that's the last step of thinking development, and then we are mature.

In the time of life when involution begins to take place, forces of regeneration are first released from the body for new thinking capacity; therefore we need a new idealism to come through our mid-life crisis. If there is no rebirth of idealism at that age to make use of these new forces and find a new balance of health, chronic disease will get worse and worse. In the next phase we see the mature social judgement of a person between fifty and sixty. A youngster judges very emotionally and personally while a mature person in his or her fifties learns to judge independently from his or her own opinion. We become good advisors because we don't project our own fantasies or judgments but really try to find what the problem is. And lastly, when the picturing forces are released in the involution of our sense organs and nervous system, we gain the wise old person's vision capacity if we have learned to use our spiritual forces. This is a most powerful task for education, to help children to activate their own faculties.

I have only been able to touch briefly on some of the questions I have received. Tomorrow I will try to address as many as I can.

Lecture 5: Questions and Answers

Thursday, February 19, 1998

Dear friends, the background of Waldorf education is the question of education and health. The theme we tried to focus on during this conference was very basic, very broad, and of course too big for so few sessions. But I hope that one or another aspect has been able to show how important it is to always have this question as a background mood for the daily work: Through what I am doing with the children, how do I affect not only their interest, their smile and activity, but also their concrete physical development. Do I really know what I am doing? We just live with the questions.

And now before I go into some thoughts to finish what we have worked on these days, I must say that I am very grateful for your questions because it's always tremendously inspiring to get questions which are a bit eye-opening. They can help me to see things which I may have brought in a way which one can misunderstand, and I can learn from this. Or they open my eyes to completely different directions that I could have thought of but didn't. And that's very helpful. On the other hand, if I have such a large package of questions, it gives me a healthy feeling of insufficiency, of not being able to do what is expected.

Dorothea Mier, who performed with her group, was very upset with me because of what I said yesterday about eurythmy, and I need to make some additional remarks to clarify what I wanted to say. Because she is occupied this morning with other obligations and cannot be here to do it herself, I promised to take her part, too, and not only clarify what I wanted to say.

Of course you could experience during the eurythmy performance and also through your own eurythmy study how important and differentiated and delicate the study of eurythmy is. You can experience, for example, that if a teacher does something like this, that this is not a eurythmy E. It is just a nice movement, isn't it? But a eurythmy A, a eurythmy E, is something very different. It is an etheric stream. And if you start to practice often and learn from Rudolf Steiner that our heart is the source of the etheric forces and that all the vowels have their origin in the heart region, you will know that you need first to pull back all your movement capacity, to bring it into silence, to bring it into pure intention, and feel that this impulse is something which has no weight but has intensity. The etheric quality has no physical weight. It flows purely in time and not in space. Our physical body with its substance and weight reveals itself in three-dimensional space. Our etheric body lives only in time. It's a system of circulations, of rhythms, of all those life cycles. It is a system of developmental laws living in time. It's the basis for the streaming changing of evolution, and this together with the physical gives what we see as the physical-etheric constitution of plants, animals, and human beings. When you study eurythmy, you have to enter into this realm of the etheric and create even physical movements out of this etheric source. You have to study for years to come into this attitude and to be able to bring movements out of the heaviness of the physical body and into this etheric lightness. And one can't do this in eurythmy without training. I did not mean that the class teacher should replace the eurythmy teacher at school. It can't be. Eurythmy is something very special.

What I did want to share, though, is a very deep concern of mine. I have lived with this concern now even in Europe, although Europe is the part of the world in which most Waldorf schools have had a eurythmy teacher. But now money is shorter than it was, and there are fewer eurythmy teachers who are really able to manage our difficult children. And so an imbalance is growing even in Germany which has always been the most fortunate country in having eurythmy in the schools. More and more schools have no eurythmy either for financial reasons or because they cannot find anybody who can manage the difficult children. And when I work with those teachers or in German teacher conferences like yours here and we speak about the specific health-bringing and pedagogical effects of eurythmy, then I realize how few of the teachers really know what eurythmy is and how it works. And therefore I always encourage teachers to study as much eurythmy as they can because doing so has three important effects. One effect is that it brings health to those who do it. It's a healthy art.

The second positive effect is that you move and use gestures much, much better. This doesn't mean that you do eurythmy in your lesson, but your spontaneous movement starts to change when you do a little bit of eurythmy every day. I say this from experience because I had the opportunity to do eurythmy in school from kindergarten through twelfth grade. Then when school was over, I really felt I was missing something, and I started to do a little eurythmy every day, and I have kept on ever since. And now when people ask me (because I don't have a strong constitution): How can you always be so busy, and how can you do this or that, why are you not tired, or how do you manage all you do although you are tired, and so on, I can always give the answer that fifty percent of this is eurythmy. I'll stop here, for I could talk for hours about the experience of living with eurythmy. It's a tremendous thing. Eurythmy has the effect that all you bring is more living because you bring it more on the basis of inner and outer movement. You learn to live in expressive movements, and this gives your own inner soul movements more flexibility and also gives your outer movements more expressiveness. Again, this doesn't mean you are doing eurythmy all the time, but that you are able to use the whole range of your movements. There is no movement you cannot find in eurythmy. This for example is the beginning of an L, done not etherically but physically. Every movement is a physical echo of eurythmic movement, and of course this expresses something.

A third, most important side effect occurs when the class teacher loves eurythmy and does even one hygienic exercise, a movement exercise with a meditation integrated, for instance in the form of a morning verse: "In my head I am light, in my limbs I am strong, in my heart I am joyful." If one does such a thing which the children then recognize in the eurythmy lesson, they will often learn eurythmy much more deeply and concretely. They will realize that the teacher whom they accept, who brings all the wisdom as class teacher, stands for eurythmy, likes eurythmy. And if the loved authority likes eurythmy, the eurythmy teacher is accepted much more easily than if the students have the feeling: Oh that's something which is a bit outside of all the other lessons, and we can enjoy it or not as we choose. If the teachers start to deepen their interest in eurythmy and its meaning for Waldorf education, then it's much easier for the eurythmy teacher to teach it, and the pupils will enter into it better. This is my concern, and I encourage teachers to do this so that eurythmy will not disappear from the schools and so that all the possibilities which are not yet seen enough, all the potential eurythmy has, can develop in the next decades. That is what I meant, and I hope I have not made any misunderstandings worse than they may already be. If you remember only: Let's love eurythmy; that would be wonderful.

Now I would like to go into the questions. I'm glad there is one dealing with the pedagogical law since what lived in me when I came here was the question of what we can do to bring this wonderful law more and more into our consciousness and our daily practice.

This request is to **discuss the pedagogical law as it applies to teachers who work with parents and children simultaneously and to those who teach adults.** We are in a sense always working with the pedagogical law because it works all the time. It is at work while I am standing here, for instance. I have to educate myself a little as I struggle to find the right words. Sometimes it's better and sometimes it's worse. You can perceive some of my self-education, and its effects go through all my sheaths. This is one aspect. You experience the other side of this. As I'm struggling, your ego feels more or less stimulated by my speech, by the way I speak and through whether the content of what I am saying reaches your *I* or not.

And the way I work with my emotions and with my gestures has an effect on your etheric constitution. You have to sit here peacefully and receive the impact of my thinking, feeling, and willing, of my movements, of my emotions, of the tone of my voice, of the astral aspects of my voice. And when you are conversing during the break, if you pay attention to how you are stimulated by others' anger or joy about something, you can feel the effect immediately. The pedagogical law is not at all theoretical, but it is a question of awareness. We are bringing to our consciousness something which works all the time. It works between adults, it works with me alone, it works between the incarnations. It is a law which stimulates all development. When a plant transforms mineral substance, this is a huge education for the mineral substance, a huge event, something new. The higher always educates and transforms the lower.

I would like to share some thoughts on what we can do to work consciously with this pedagogical law. **How can we school our ego to work well with the astral of the other person, specifically of the student? What can we do for our astral so that it works best with the student's etheric, and how can we lead our etheric to work better with their physical constitution?** There is one big difference between working with children and working with adults. The ego forces of children are not yet free, so they do not yet have enough distance to protect their constitution from my influence. As an adult I can distance myself with the forces of my *I*, with my intellectual thinking. Of course I am exposed to what is going on, but I can do a lot inwardly to protect myself from many of these influences. Even when I am attacked, I can immediately mobilize my soul, for example by thinking: That is not right, or I will not take it now, I will think about it later. I can work with this attack. The child, however, is open and must take it in. The child does not

yet have the ability through the power of self-education to protect him- or herself. The pedagogical law was given for those
children who have less ego capacity than normal ones do, the
children who need curative education, who have many more
problems than those children we have in school. But because in
our schools now more and more children enter with a certain
weakness of their forces, this pedagogical law becomes more
and more relevant for us all to work with consciously.

There is one magic word for strengthening our ego capacity wherever we go, and that is *identification.* The power of identification is the purest experience of our *I* forces. Only the ego
can say: I am I. This is the sentence of identification. It is a very
special thing. If we say *I am I,* then we experience our self as it
is. Whether we like it or dislike it, we have no choice, we must
take ourselves as we are. The starting point is that we name
this crazy thing: I. And then the business comes of questioning,
asking: Who am I? Why am I? What am I? Am I really the person of today, or am I more the person I was twenty years ago,
or will I arrive at my true being twenty years in the future?
Many many questions. We can question ourselves and that's
interesting. We exist, and at the same time we can question
ourselves as if we did not exist. There is a huge tension between
questioning ourselves (non-identification) and answering
(identification). This is the mystery of the *I*, pictured in the
ancient alchemical symbol of the snake biting its own tail.

At last through all the questioning comes the confirmation:
This is me. This is what I want, this is what I stand for, this is
my life ideal, this is my true self. What we do out of our own
activity in this second process, this step of confirmation and
identification, is the creation we add to God's creation. This
wonderful act is the second birth we have to do ourselves.
Through the pain of questioning we bring ourselves to birth
once more, and a new identity, a new security arises by this act
of identification. And if we now teach something, this mystery
of the ego is always behind us. We teach—let me say it very
starkly—in an *I*-less, an ego-less way if we teach a subject we
are not identified with. Then the pedagogical law has a terrible

effect on the children. My experience is that the more a teacher has consciously identified with and has questioned through his subjects—not only teaching because he knows everything, but really having brought his subject a bit through this process of questioning why do I like this, what is the importance and relevance for today—the more the children will listen and understand. Then our ego power has a good effect on the student's astral which is active in thinking, feeling, and willing. I would like to give you three very little examples of how this is meant.

If you deal with numbers in math, how can you yourself identify with numbers? They seem rather abstract at first. Bear in mind that this act of identification that I am speaking of is preparation for the teacher and is not what you would teach the children. What you can teach of it depends on the age, on the question, and so forth. But for yourself it is necessary that you really look and question where we deal with numbers in life, in technology, in creation, in music. Numbers are the most selfless rulers of everything. Therefore they can also be greatly misused. Anyone can do anything with numbers. You can plan a war with numbers and you can plan most joyful strategies with numbers. You make money with numbers. Numbers are—and this is most helpful if we study Anthroposophy—a gift of the cherubim, of the spirits of harmony. Our whole world is thoroughly harmonized and worked through with numbers. Then one might focus on the different qualities of numbers. What is a one; a two, a polarity; a three, balance between polarities; a four, the stabilization of a process; and then this five which brings disorder and was always the number of crisis and of evil—interesting things, just to show how one can enter such a process of identification with a subject. And if the students feel numbers are something the teacher really loves and lives with, they will understand every math operation better.

Or for chemistry you might enter into the mystery of transubstantiation, of transformation of substance. Or you could look into the system of the elements based on laws of music, those eight groups built up like an octave. Or you can take history, and if you only teach who lived here or there, or tell fairy tales from the past without considering whether it reaches your own understanding as a human being, it will not be working with the meaning of this pedagogical law. I think this is your daily bread and that I don't need to say more.

This mystery of identification is the key to bringing the ego power into the lesson with full concentration and love. Identification is purest love, and love is the most powerful expression of ego capacity. If we have this ego capacity, then this thought of love is at the same time identity with truth, with real understanding. You can only identify if you try as much as possible to understand. And if your love for the subject is so strong that you let the subject live, and if you give space so that the subject may reveal itself, then you give freedom, you educate towards freedom, this quality of love which is not an astral feeling, but which is ego power. If in this love lives a true understanding or the will to understand, and if this love carries this giving space so that others can develop, then the subject can appear. Freedom is not something we use but is something that we give or share. The will aspect of love is freedom, the knowledge aspect of love is truth and understanding, and the feeling aspect of love is love. Love is the powerful attitude of identification, and in this attitude, when we get up in the morning, we ask ourselves: How can I love what I have to bring today. And maybe we will find a new little touch to feel closer to it.

There is another magic word to help us get our astral ready to educate, and this is *flexibility*. Our astral body is a rhythmic, moving body which carries the wisdom of the feelings, the wisdom of music, but which also brings everything to consciousness. It is the awakener of everything and is that which makes us sensitive. We need our astral body to make thoughts, feelings, and will activities conscious for our inner life, for the astral is the carrier of our conscious soul life of thinking, feeling, and willing. Although the power of thoughts comes out of the etheric and the power of will comes out of the ego, these activities live consciously in the soul which is carried by this flexible astral body. The astral can adapt to everything and can internalize so that we experience an inner space of soul awareness, of consciousness. Flexibility is the magic word for the astral because everything we meet has different sides. In French there is a nice proverb: *toute médaille a son revers*—every medal has two sides. And that is typical for the astral. The astral body lives between sympathy and antipathy. It is a huge movement to come from sympathy into the opposite pole of antipathy. It is in the astral that we have this constant tension between polarities and have to live flexibly in between. While you are sitting here, for example, thinking that it's good that you're here, your children at home may be suffering that you are gone. They experience the other side of the same event. This conference has a good and a bad side. And of course if you stay at home, the bad side is that you are not here. So you can do what you want, you will always have positive and negative aspects. Through Anthroposophy we learn that there are more than two aspects, but I will leave that out for now.

We start with at least two aspects to train ourselves to become flexible in our souls. And if we have to meet twenty or twenty-five or even thirty children, or forty in some European schools, then you have to be enormously flexible because children react very differently. Some are excited by what you are bringing, others find it boring, a third group doesn't listen, and you must embrace all these different movements with your astral body without having the prejudice or expectation that all the children must be excited, for example. Of course, if you work like this, more and more they will all be excited because they will feel understood, regarded, accepted, integrated. But this is an enormous process and requires great effort on your part. For instance, if you have some students who can't enter into the lesson, you do not say to yourself without thinking: Oh they are ill, or: They are stupid. Rather, you really investigate and make the reason for a certain behavior a question of research until you have understood their provocation, their situation. Then you will be able to integrate them. This requires a huge flexibility in your emotional life because antipathy toward difficult children closes the door to a true understanding. The problem of the astral is that we are quickly offended. The danger is that we lose our flexibility and just close. We often observe that in puberty people go through a time when they don't speak for some days with one another because they are completely upset and offended. The astral lives in movement and looks from different sides in a constant act of adaptation. It is very helpful just to realize that my astral body loves flexibility, my ego loves identification. I have to work to foster this

The etheric is the selfless realm of habits and of longlasting constant *rhythm*. Our etheric body is not at all spontaneous—that's the astral with its flexibility. The etheric is very, very boring and always repeats the same thing. If we are healthy, we can be glad that it repeats our health, that it controls all the organs' functions which must be repeated, repeated, repeated. This service of life by nurturing, by repeating, by taking care of the time, by punctually starting and ending the lessons to keep the rhythms is very helpful. Having rituals helps a lot to strengthen the children's and your own etheric body. If you have a certain ritual of standing at the door in the morning, greeting the children a specific way, having some activities that you do every morning, the children love it, and they will miss these rituals if you don't do them. Look for such nice little things for the beginning and the end, customs which the children love and take to strengthen their physical body and which for you are a permanent strengthening of your etheric body. And always bring into the morning verse, which is such a regular rhythmic little ritual, as much identification, flexibility, and good rhythm as possible so that you can make this etheric imprint powerful.

The key word for the physical body is *joy*. After this week's branch evening some friends came to me because I praised the Sophia. She is a being whom we can reach through imitating her. Sophia has to suffer before she can bear a child, she has to be in the desert, as it is described in the Apocalypse of St. John, before she can receive the human being. The dragon has to be overcome before true wisdom is gained, and so on. This is a path through pain to joy. Joy exists directly and without pain, but this is not Sophia. So we discussed this matter a little. In his earliest lectures about education Rudolf Steiner gives only this key word regarding the physical body: The physical body will grow healthily through joy, through every smile of the teacher, through every nice gesture of the mother. Joy is the atmosphere in which physical organs can grow.

For us adults it is quite difficult at times to achieve a certain amount of joy in existence, even the joy that we are still here and able to see the sun, the sky, the flowers, joy in thinking about events and people we love and like, maybe joy in remembering that we have an angel who protects us and is with us except in those moments when we have to learn something. At those times he must lift his wings a little bit so that suffering can come when we need it, but he keeps all the other sufferings away. We don't have to suffer, we only see it in others. So we search for strategies to bring this element of joy into our life so that the physical body of the students can meet this atmosphere. Learning and being flexible is Sophia and always causes a little pain. We have to overcome ourselves, we have to forgive, we might feel the bitterness of being unjustly accused. This is the threshold of pain. The etheric is the realm of thought and the physical is the realm of joy of existence, and the ego is this realm of identification and the will to learn and transform.

That's the drama we are in, and we can be helped through the guiding motifs of identification, flexibility, rhythm, and joy, to remember what children want to meet aside from the subjects and class activities. These qualities educate and stimulate the child and give him the certainty that it is worth becoming a human being because it is exciting to experience it in the form of this wonderful teacher. That is really the best we can do because quite often children do not have such examples of adults at home, and educators often need to supply the father and mother qualities in school.

That is what I wanted to give as a conclusion to this pedagogical law. Now I will enter this flower bucket of questions!

There were some questions dealing with the **attention deficit syndrome**, this ADD, and also one reminding us of the theory that it's not an attention deficiency but that it is an over-focusing of attention. If we look at the history of this syndrome, the hyperkinetic syndrome, attention deficit syndrome, and there are other names you may know, there have been different theories for understanding it. The first theories treated it as a learning problem, a developmental problem, and a bit of a moral failure, so one always attacked these children: "Sit better" and "behave better" and "how naughty you are," and the children always felt blamed morally. Such a theory was not helpful for these children, of course. A lot of research has been done, and there was a shift at the end of this century to the theory that this disorder is an imbalance of the neuro-transmitter system of the brain, the overstimulation or understimulation of certain neuro-transmitters. The overstimulation theory of attention is based on this over- and understimulation of the neuro-transmitters.

All these theories and aspects are viewpoints which can help to understand what's going on, but for us as educators and doctors, the good thing is that the pedagogical strategy is always the same, independent of all theories. The strategy concerns those children who are not able to enter with their attention into the program we have, children who have lots of strength, lots of will power, lots of energy, but who can't control it so that it fits into our programs, who appear occupied with many things but very rarely with those we want.

The strategy is first to understand such a constitution, to see that there is a strong will and intensity and power for doing something, and a lack of control and guidance. To help, we must find a strategy of very little steps, and the steps must be so small that the child has the good feeling: I can manage this. If you read books on ADD and they are good, then you find examples like this: A boy with ADD leaves the bathroom in chaos every morning, and his mother and sister complain about it every morning, and this boy starts his day with this blame: I'm naughty and insufficient and it's always the same and I can't, I can't.

And this is the secret: Does this boy refuse to do better, or is he rather unable to—won't he or can't he? And we as educators must always say to ourselves: Every child wants to develop, wants to learn something. Waldorf education is based on this premise. Children come to school to become human beings, to learn for their life, for their self-development. So if they provoke, if they seem not to be willing, this must be telling us that they really cannot, and we must find out why. The basis of psychiatric treatment for children and the basis for school doctors' conversations with teachers is then that one devises individual learning strategies for children who cannot enter our normal program, who need special pathways to gain control of their capacities.

And so one can read further. A contract was made with this boy saying very nicely: Of course you want to, but now you cannot because your constitution has such an energy that it is more difficult for you than for others to bring it under control. So we have made a nice map on the door of the bathroom and a beautiful checklist with nice pictures. First: is the sink clean, did you arrange your toothbrush, did you remove the white spots, did you close the toilet seat, did you pick up your towel from the floor after your shower and hang it on the rack? Everything is on this wonderful checklist, and at the top before opening the door to leave is: Please check. This wonderfully, intelligently thought-out checklist ends with: I've checked, and the boy comes out and the bathroom is clean. This is just an example, but it is very important to realize that behind many so-called impossibilities or naughtinesses or inefficiencies is the fact that these children or youngsters are unable on their own to understand the message and to find for themselves such small steps that they really can accomplish.

I'll give another example from my experience. At the beginning of a high school main lesson, during the morning verse, one youngster started to work in the bag containing all his school things. There he was, rummaging about while the class was saying the morning verse which is so important. And as I stood there, I felt this anger coming up in myself. After the verse was finished we began the lesson, and when the young people started to work by themselves, I went to this boy and told him I would talk to him in the break—I said this not in a very nice tone. And he asked me: Why? I told him: You did all sorts of things during the morning verse; I was very upset about this. And then he looked at me with very nice brilliant astonished eyes, saying: Is that true? I didn't realize that. This was a very delicate moment in which I thought: Shall I trust him or not? (It's eleventh grade!) And I decided to trust him, and I said: Well if you really didn't realize that, I trust you, then pay attention tomorrow, and maybe don't put your bag on the desk, put it below. And the interesting experience for me was that after this short conversation I had a good relationship to this boy for the rest of that course. From this moment on he had the ability to listen to what I said.

For me the message in this experience was that we are surrounded by many provocations and problems, but behind them is a pure and often shy and unable person who wants to do better but can't and really needs the help of little steps, and primarily the help of trust and understanding. It is helpful to look for a conversation in which to find a strategy with this boy or girl on the basis of this trust: I know that you want to do better but that you can't out of physical or soul or whatever reasons, but I will help you. Let us try to find out together what is the best strategy. This also helps to build up a personal relationship which many youngsters today need for their development because they haven't yet experienced it.

This ADD syndrome is a challenge to us to meet the best will of the child and to be open for little conferences with, if it's possible, a school doctor, or a psychologist who treats the child, the parents, some teachers, and the child itself, to work out good strategies lesson by lesson. Sometimes, if for example there are five or six children of that sort in the class, this isn't possible. It is therefore more and more important to integrate therapeutic circles into the school, circles made up of interested parents who have time to spend or people from the local branch who want to help, and these volunteer helpers can take one of these children for an hour or half an hour and work with them one on one while allowing the class to relax a little. It is not a solution to expel these children and it is not a solution to drug them so much that they just sit there. We must find a healthy balance, and I think we increasingly need the help in school of people who stand around such a class with the will to balance problems at least for a few months. Often such a crisis turns after two, three, or four months, and then the help isn't necessary any more.

There were some questions about diseases which are on the rise, such as asthma or allergies. The medicine of our time has most wonderful results, and we must say emphatically that people in our time live longer than has ever been possible before in human development. So this medicine can't be bad; it must be good. The physical body can survive much longer than in earlier times. But the problem is that this sort of care has a bad side effect in that we know how to take care of the physical body from the outside but we lose the knowledge of how to take care of the physical body from the inside. And therefore we now see more illnesses which come from a lack of activity, from a lack of trust in the body's own forces.

Anthroposophical medicine is an amplification of mainstream medicine which adds to this wonderful knowledge about the physical body the knowledge of the spiritual bodies. So we only use the help from the physical side when it is absolutely necessary and instead encourage as much as possible the body's own forces of regeneration. We don't use vaccination, antibiotics, and stimulation for this and that. For instance, it is absolutely stupid to drink milk containing vitamin D every morning—as I have done while I've been here. Well, don't blame me, but of course it weakens me a little. My body is accustomed to producing its own vitamin D with the light and the minerals I eat. For babies the situation is different. One must look. In Europe with our dark woods it might be useful, but here in California where you have the sunshine day after day it isn't, not yet. For me it's a wonder why even this vitamin which is produced by everybody oneself on one's own if one has enough sunshine, is added here in the milk. This is just a silly example.

Everything the body receives without activity weakens it and makes it less active. Every human being when it gets something gratis, takes it without activity. The good side is you have it without energy, and the bad side is that you have not trained your energy. So now because we protect the immune system from any big challenge, we have lots of allergies very simply because the immune system isn't trained enough. And so for me it's not at all a wonder that these problems increase. They must increase. I'm very happy that many doctors in Europe, but I think also here, are starting to think this through afresh and sing the song: The immune system needs good stimulation. Identification and positive moods help to stimulate the immune system, as does learning to fight, through the body's own forces of self-regeneration, against effects from outside. Of course we need to find the right balance in this.

Then there's the question of whether we should accept students who are on Ritalin. Of course we accept all students who are brought and whom we can manage in the class. And if Waldorf education works well and if the child loves his teacher, Ritalin becomes unnecessary. This drug can be very helpful, but if it is taken too long, it can be the first drug to which a child becomes accustomed, and then it gives the inclination to use other drugs later to stimulate soul and will capacity—and this cannot be intended. So we as doctors struggle always to find the right strategy, to do what we can to encourage the child's own capacity for equilibration, for example with those strategies with little steps—but if the child is for the moment unable to do this, we might prescribe Ritalin for a certain amount of time. However, before I or any good doctor would do this, I would start first with a little cup of coffee. Coffee quite often has the same effect as Ritalin, and its intrusion into the metabolism of the brain is not as deep. Try a nice little cup of coffee. The children are then a bit like the adults, they go to business, they have their coffee so that they can work better, and then this is sometimes help enough together with a good strategy.

I received questions concerning children under the influence of alcohol either at birth or during pregnancy, and children born from an extracorporal conception. More and more children come out of such conceptions, and I can really only say: Take care of every human being who wants your help. The greater the difficulties are, the more our therapeutic involvement should develop. We learn through these children to become better teachers and better human beings, and we must try to find out what we can do for them depending on the needs of the children in our care.

I know children out of extracorporal fertilization who appear totally like other children, and I know others who appear very difficult, but I must say I also know extremely difficult children coming out of normal fertilization. So I can't say this is impossible. I do not wish now to appear as a promoter of extracorporal fertilization, don't misunderstand me. A lot speaks against it. These methods have a fifteen percent success rate, and quite often eighty to eighty-five percent failure, so one can see that this is a constitution which is very delicate. But if parents decide to take this way, and if a child accepts this sort of fertilization, and if the parents then look for a Waldorf school, we should be ready to look forward to meeting this child and to making the very best out of the situation.

And now a few questions about rhythm. One question concerns the relative benefits of three-week and four-week blocks. Twenty-four hours is the rhythm of the ego. Seven days is the rhythm of reaction, health reaction, reaction to attacks, the rhythm of the astral. Four times seven to bring a good reaction into habit is the rhythm of the etheric. And one year is the rhythm of the growth and establishment of the physical body.

So if one wants to reach not only the astral but also the etheric so that the occupation with a certain content in thoughts and feelings really goes into the etheric, one needs to change and reorganize the subjects into longer, four-week blocks. Of course we have more subjects than blocks—that's a very easy count. But if we want to reach the etheric, which is very important, then we need to find a new order for the subjects and follow an indication that Rudolf Steiner gave for all the subjects to put them together in a way which would allow different subjects to contribute to the understanding of one content.

There is a most beautiful example of how this is meant in the seventh-grade block on health education. Steiner suggests that this health block be taught together with the study of economic life. If one studies the routes of products—how does the milk come from the cow to the ice cream, and so forth—this is nothing other than the projection of good digestion. In a healthily functioning organism, all the products, all the substances, all the elements of nutrition find their way to where they are needed in the quantities needed. And a good economic life provides what a society really needs and should not provide what is not needed. This is a tremendously inspiring way to teach economics, bringing it together with the functioning of health in the human organism. Then also one has to count and deal with numbers in economic life and in the health life, so one can bring math in a bit as well as some physics. And one can then see whether in the physics block one can bring those aspects of physics into memory again which were introduced in the health block, and this refreshes and shortens the physics block.

At teachers' conferences it would be wonderful to sit together to discover how we can design new blocks for different subjects, because a block is more interesting the more parts of life it integrates for the student. And four weeks of only math is boring!—at least for me it was. But if other interesting things are integrated, the whole thing is more enlivened, and one really reaches the etheric in this time. This is only possible if we can find new blocks.

And then if there are a few odd weeks left as there often are before holidays, it is good to take seven or fourteen days as a kind of astral refreshment, a short one-week block which is very well prepared and interestingly taught. And if the students know from the beginning that there is only one week for this tremendously interesting subject, it gives them a stimulus and a certain glimpse into the subject, and it will not be forgotten. That's an astral effect. And if what is brought in this short block reappears here and there in the other blocks, then this is a good change and balance and is productive use of these smaller bits of time.

And it is very important to take care of the physical body through these rhythms too. At the beginning and at the end of the year it is good to reflect: What do we want to do in this year? and at the end: What did we learn? This is something like a birthday meditation: I'm one year older now, how was the last year, what will I learn next year? One can do something similar with the year's events, and using the festivals of the year to celebrate this rhythm also gives a stabilization for the physical body. Also daily rituals and weekly rituals, specifically in the early grades, are very helpful for encouraging a healthy reactive rhythm and help to bring the quality of each day into the consciousness of the child.

And then there's the topic of the five-day week. When I asked Joan Almon whether we should address at the upcoming Kolisko conference the impact of the five-day rhythm and how to overcome it, she laughed at me and said: This theme is out in the United States; you can't change our five-day week. So we have not integrated this theme into the Kolisko Conference. But of course if one has a five-day week, it is important to see that such a weekly rhythm is made up of two days (Saturday-Sunday) and then five days (Monday-Friday). This is not an ideal rhythm because it has no archetype in the constitution. It is not the best we can do. Just knowing this is important, and maybe one can speak with interested parents who might then arrange, for example, that on Saturdays the children in the family get up as they do on school days and do their weekend homework in the morning, creating a kind of school morning at home. Or several children might gather at one home to do this together. And then the weekend really starts at noon on Saturday.

Such a simple thing done by some parents can already bring a change towards a seven-day rhythm. If one has six days and then a one-day break, this stabilizes the rhythm. Every rhythm has a beginning and an end, and so on the Sunday or seventh day it is very important to have nothing. This is an important stabilizer to keep the rhythm elastic. Beat does not carry life. All life rhythms are irregular, and through a certain irregularity they become elastic. The more flexible our body's rhythmic system is, the more adaptable our body is in the face of attacks. This adaptivity is a question of the breathing of irregularity in these rhythms, and if you have beat, then you have a rhythm which is not at all flexible. For example, if the heart starts to beat too steadily, then a cardiologist knows that the risk of death is tremendously higher than if we are experiencing a rhythmic disorder after a heart attack. In that case the heart is looking for a new elasticity for its own rhythm. Therefore to do something for six days and then have a day of something different is necessary to stimulate a nice carrying flexible rhythm. Of course for adults these things are different. I am speaking now about how to establish a healthy constitution for children.

Now I will just touch on a couple of questions about teeth. If the teeth appear too early or too late, this usually has nothing to do with the maturity of the white part of the teeth. This dentine part grows and develops and regenerates like a bone and is therefore something different. But the part of the teeth which does not regenerate matures between six and eight years regardless of whether the teeth are still in the jaw or are already out or even if they are behind the first teeth and have to wait for them to be removed by the dentist. What these irregularities mean for the child's constitution is a special chapter, but from the angle of intelligence that I spoke about, this birth of the etheric, it does not have much to say. When this white part of the teeth mineralizes and gets ready is the time when the etheric forces are being liberated from this part of the body. And of course we have some children who are more intelligent than others. To have the maturity of teeth is not a guarantee that we are brilliant intellectual memorizers, as we all know.

And now a last question regarding what my husband shared last year about these **fifty minutes, the rhythm of the moon, and the lesson which is forty-five minutes long.** Of course it would be better to have fifty minutes for a lesson if one really wants to reach and to activate the will. But three quarters of an hour is already the threshold to reach the will because minutes are the rhythms of emotions and everything which goes over half an hour is already from the rhythm aspect disposed to reach the will. The best would be to start on time and to end fifty minutes later, but depending on the age of the child and the attention capacity, one must bring the subject in different forms so that an artistic element and an intellectual element and an element of doing comes and goes in the right fashion.

I would like to end with this, although I really must beg your pardon because some questions have not yet been touched on. There were some special questions regarding different illnesses. From the aspect of **physical health** we have the magic word: **Activity!** The physical body needs to be active and not passively served; it must move itself and not only be driven in a car, and so on. But to prevent all the disturbances of soul and spirit we also need to find a way to bring the human being's soul and spiritual forces into real activity. The more human beings can use and control their own activity, the healthier they are in body, soul, and spirit. So everything I wanted to bring can be summed up: Let us think from all sides how to wake up a child's own activity, and let us stimulate this activity through our own enthusiasm and activity.

This is the only strategy I know to prevent from the very beginning all forms of addiction and abuse. Addiction and abuse are symptoms of dissatisfaction. People don't feel as they want to feel: enjoying an active, meaningful existence, having relationships, having their pain but being able to work with it. These symptoms indicate that many people of our time have difficulties finding themselves. They are not bad people, but are people who have not had good conditions to develop in. Or maybe their conditions have been too good, hindering them from strengthening enough their own activity to learn. So we try to find strategies to reach the most inner ego force, to reach the will, to develop it with attention. I would say that to love the child's will and to help him find his own way into self and world experience is the aim of our pedagogical challenge.

Notes on the Illustrations

The six human embryo pictures by Dr. Erich Blechschmidt published in *Der menschliche Embryo* (Stuttgart: F.K. Schattauer Verlag GmbH) are reproduced with the kind permission of Frau Dr. Blechschmidt.

The four microscopic sections of the human cerebrum are from Helma Thielscher-Noll and Hans Gerhard Noll, *Das Eltern-Seminar, Erziehen und Begleiten bis zum 10. Lebensjahr,* Verlag Gesundheit, 1996.

The picture and skeleton of the jumping mouse are from Wolfgang Schad, *Säugetiere und Mensch Zur Gestaltbiologie vom Gesichtspunkt der Dreigliederung,* Stuttgart: Verlag Freies Geistesleben, 1971.

The picture of human and animal limb forms is from Thomas McKeen, *Wesen und Gestalt des Menschen,* Stuttgart: Verlag Freies Geistesleben, 1996.

The profiles of the chimpanzee at three stages of development are from *Goetheanistische Naturwissenschaft,* Vol 4 *Anthropologie,* Wolfgang Schad, ed., Stuttgart: Verlag Freies Geistesleben, 1985.

The graph showing organ growth from birth to age twenty is from *Einführung in die Entwicklungsphysiologie des Kindes* Heinrich Wiesener, ed., Berlin—Göttingen—Heidelberg: Springer Verlag, 1964.

The graphs on pages 54, 56, 57, and 58 are the work of Gunther Hildebrandt, published in Michaela Glöckler, *Gesundheit und Schule,* Dornach: Verlag am Goetheanum, 1998.